ACTIVE LIFE, PASSIVE INCOME

ACTIVE LIFE PASSIVE INCOME

ACHIEVE FINANCIAL INDEPENDENCE THROUGH REAL ESTATE INVESTING

Nate Lambert, PhD

HOUNDSTOOTH
PRESS

ACTIVE LIFE, PASSIVE INCOME
Achieve Financial Independence through Real Estate Investing

ISBN 978-1-5445-1978-4 *Hardcover*
      978-1-5445-1977-7 *Paperback*
      978-1-5445-1976-0 *Ebook*

TO MY WIFE, FOR BEING MY BIGGEST
SOURCE OF SUPPORT AND INSPIRATION.

CONTENTS

PART III: NUTS AND BOLTS OF THE DEAL

PART IV: BUILDING AND PROTECTING

PART V: A SUCCESS MINDSET

DISCLAIMERS

I am not a licensed attorney, accountant, financial advisor, broker, or any other licensed individual. Therefore, I will not discuss or provide any specific counsel, advice, or instruction that would apply to specific individuals. The information in this book is intended to be general information and is not intended to replace the advice of professionals. I recommend you engage the services of professionals in making decisions that have a legal impact, especially financial decisions.

There are several examples cited in the book showing how money was made by applying the principles described. This in no way is a representation of a typical result or the result every person will experience. Real estate investment results depend upon a variety of factors unique to each opportunity. The examples do not guarantee or predict a similar result in any past, present, or future real estate investment opportunities. Each real estate investment result is as unique as the real estate itself.

INTRODUCTION

"You're not a fit for our department," my new boss informed me during our second conversation. He had voted against me, but enough of the other faculty had voted yes that I got what I thought was my dream job as a professor of family psychology. Now it felt like the rug had been pulled out from under me. My new department chair was dead set on making sure that I wouldn't be staying there for long now that he had the power. My job was in jeopardy.

I was never good at having a boss, but from day one, this guy seemed to have decided that sabotaging my career was his top priority. We butted heads constantly, and no matter how well I taught or how many journal articles I published, it was never about that. It was about him winning. It had all culminated in this moment.

It had been a tough journey to become a professor. I had spent nine years of my life getting my PhD, and during that time, my family lived on a $14,000 a year salary, far below the poverty level. We even had to get food stamps. Once I got my dream job, I spent countless hours researching, writing, and publishing journal articles. In just my third year as a professor, I had published seventy-two peer-reviewed journal articles, which is almost unheard of and which was more than most of the professors in my department who had been around for thirty-plus years. But my family was still struggling financially. My wife was a full-time mom, and I was supporting our young family of five boys with a small salary and only one car.

Now I was at a crossroads. Would I put it all on the line to fight for my career as a professor? Or would I risk it all to recreate myself, going in a completely different direction to pursue my newfound passion in real estate? Did I have the courage to put my loved ones at risk to cut off the golden handcuffs? It would require that I walk into the darkness into a 100 percent commission-based career with no past evidence of success.

It was terrifying, but I took those first steps into the darkness. Five years later, my life had completely transformed. No longer is my family struggling to get by. We have a second car now—my dream car, a Tesla Model S—as well as our dream home, a nine-thousand-square-foot mansion in the foothills of the mountains. In 2019, I spent three months of the year on vacation, building priceless memories with my family, and I still made more money than ever before!

Looking back now, I'm grateful for that boss who hated me. He made my life hell, but he also gave me the final push I needed to cut off the golden handcuffs and begin enjoying true freedom.

THE POWER OF DISSATISFACTION

Every journey on the road to success begins with dissatisfaction. If you're completely satisfied with everything in your life, you won't be motivated to push for greater heights of achievement. Are you 100 percent satisfied with your career right now?

I was a good professor. In addition to my numerous publications, I received invitations from around the world to places like Israel, England, and Australia to present my research. I had an international reputation! I had published five books, including one, titled *Publish and Prosper*, showing other professors how to write and publish more than they thought possible. Just three years in, I was already set for my entire career. Beyond my publications, I worked hard to be an extraordinary mentor. I love to teach, and I helped dozens of students learn the publishing process. I worked collaboratively with them so that they could get experience in researching and earn authorship on my publications. In this way, I was able to delegate and build a massive body of publications while simultaneously helping to launch the careers of many students.

Most people in this kind of position would be very satisfied, yet I was not. I was bored and tired of the stress of living paycheck to paycheck. I didn't like being someone else's servant, and I didn't feel like I was making much of an impact on the world. In short, I was suffering from the same four sources of dissatisfaction that so many of us struggle with: no fun, no money, no freedom, no impact.

NO FUN

I am a people person, and as a professor I was cooped up in my office all day writing research articles. It was boring. I tried to divert myself into my new yard and planted a massive garden and fifty-three fruit trees. While I enjoyed this work, it was only a few hours of fun, with the vast majority of my time still spent chained to my desk. Eventually, I completed all my home projects and was left with nothing but the boredom of my day-to-day job.

What about you? Do you wake up each day excited to go to work? Or has your desk become a prison cell, where you count down the hours until you can leave?

NO MONEY

Professors don't make very much money, so my family and I lived a *very* frugal lifestyle. We could afford only one car, which my wife needed to transport the kids, so I rode my bike to work, regardless of whether it was one hundred degrees or minus ten. About the only place we could afford to eat out was McDonald's. We never bought an actual meal; we just purchased several of the ninety-nine-cent burgers so we could keep the bill under ten dollars. Though I love to travel, we rarely did. It was simply impossible to go to most of the places I wanted because money was *so* tight.

Even with the constant skimping and saving, I was under constant financial pressure. We were living paycheck to paycheck, and I wondered what would happen to my family in case of an emergency. I wouldn't have the means to pay for it.

The most frustrating part was that my pay wasn't correlated to my performance. It didn't matter how well I did in my job; my income was fixed with a 1 to 2 percent raise per year. Though I had outstanding performance reviews, I was not rewarded with a higher income.

Do you have the financial independence to do the things you want? Are you living paycheck to paycheck, worried about how to provide comfort and security for your family?

NO FREEDOM

One of the worst aspects of my job was feeling like I was someone else's servant. I had to get permission for everything, and as I mentioned, my department chair hated me, which was a major problem, since my fate and future as a professor was largely in his hands. He could talk crap about me to the senior professors and ultimately get me terminated. I dreamed of one day being my own boss and calling the shots for my own business. No longer would I need to get permission for something as simple as going out of town, or grovel before someone I did not even like. Maintaining job security meant I had no choice but to follow the system.

Who controls your time: you or your boss? Do you have the freedom to make your own decisions, or are you stuck in a bureaucratic system? Are you tired of always being told what to do, how to do it, and when?

NO IMPACT

So much of what I was going through may have been worth it if I felt like I was really having a positive impact on the world. Yet I found out the average journal article is read by three people outside of the author. I was busting my butt to reach three people who were probably other researchers like me. How could I impact people in the real world? It didn't seem like I was doing much good for anyone, and this irked me. I knew I could help a small group of my students, but I longed to make a real difference, and my employment was not getting me there.

What kind of real-world impact do you want to make? Does your job empower you to do it?

Faced with all this dissatisfaction, I finally decided I wanted out. I wanted freedom—not just financial independence but also the freedom to do work I enjoyed, to make my own decisions, and to have the impact I wanted. I read a book, much like this one, that explained how passive income through real estate investing could lead to financial independence, and I was hooked. I knew I had to start taking action if I wanted to change the direction of my life, and I was ready to do anything to become a real estate investor. This new journey captured my attention because it presented a solution to the woes I was experiencing as a professor.

WHY REAL ESTATE AS THE PATH TO FREEDOM?

You may ask, why is real estate *the* path to freedom? Of all the reasons, these three are the most important:

#1: IT'S EASIER TO TRAVEL THE BEATEN PATH

Could you make a lot of money by starting a successful business and selling it? Yes, but 95 percent of new businesses fail in the first five years. The amount of work you put in for something that will likely not take off can be enormous. The path to wealth in real estate is well traveled, and success leaves clues. Like any reputable profession, you must get educated and have a mentor to guide you, but real estate isn't rocket science. Almost anybody can learn and succeed at it.

#2: YOU CAN USE OTHER PEOPLE'S MONEY TO BUILD WEALTH

You have probably heard "It takes money to make money." This is absolutely true! With most investments, like stocks, you need to have a ton of money up front to make serious cash. You need money in real estate as well, but it doesn't need to be *your* money. In fact, I rarely use my own money for my many fix and flips. Recently, I had fourteen flips going on, which required $4.5 million to buy and rehab. I didn't use a dime of my own cash, and I made crazy-high returns! With this ability to use other people's money, the barrier to entry is open to anyone who is willing to learn how to find good deals. The money will flow to the deal as you build relationships with key people.

#3: YOU CAN USE OTHER PEOPLE'S TIME

This one is *most* important for true freedom. Many people who get into real estate investing trade one job for another.

They're swinging the hammer in a flip, finding the tenants, fixing the toilet at midnight, and cursing everyone who told them real estate is a dream. Do not fall into that trap! A business that sets you free is one that allows you the time to have a blast in Europe with your family for a month while your business keeps working for you while you're gone! To have an active life, you need *passive income*—income that comes in each month with minimal effort from you and allows you to live your life the way you want.

I *suck* with construction and never swing any hammers, even though I'm a major house flipper. My lack of skill has been a blessing to me, as it has kept me focused on my true job, which is simply to coordinate everything. There is enough profit available in real estate that there's no reason not to hire a professional to do all the work for you. They will do a much better job than you could ever do yourself, as they bring expertise to the table. At this point, there are only three things I really do: (1) find deals, (2) arrange money, and (3) manage construction crews—other people do almost everything else for me! In fact, I rarely even find deals myself anymore.

The chance to travel a beaten path, to make a fortune with other people's money, and to delegate almost all tasks makes real estate the best possible path for financial independence. It allows you to be able to do what you want, when you want, where you want, with whom you want, and for how long you want.

HOW TO USE THIS BOOK

I designed this book for people who are where I was ten years ago: people who want more—more money, more time, more freedom, more fun, more impact—but feel stuck. Maybe you're burned out at your job. Maybe you're tired of working fifty weeks a year for two weeks of vacation. Maybe you dream of the opportunity to really help people and live at a higher level but don't know if you can do it.

I'm here to tell you that you can. The only thing holding you back is knowledge.

A lot of people I know are interested in real estate investing. They listen to podcasts and read about it, but they never end up making the jump to actually *doing* it. They've heard too many horror stories of people losing their shirts in real estate and are afraid of making a mistake that will set them back. I understand that fear—I've felt it myself. To get over that fear, you need guidance and a mentor, and that is what I seek to provide with this book.

This book is not a detailed step-by-step guide on how to complete every awkward step of a real estate deal—you can figure all of that out online and through practice. Rather, the purpose of this book is to give you a vision of what is possible and provide a strategy guide and a foundation of knowledge to get you started on your journey. In these pages, I will take you through the common mistakes to avoid and the strategies and tactics that lead to success, so that you can build the confidence you need to begin your own real estate investing career. My goal is to fill in the blanks and give you what is missing in every other real estate book out there.

I've divided this book into five parts. The first part, Vision and Strategy, covers the high-level, foundational beliefs and strategies needed to build a freedom-based real estate career. The second part, Finding the Money, dives into the different ways you can purchase properties, and then the third part, Nuts and Bolts of the Deal, explains the strategies and tactics of completing deals. Next, the fourth part, Building and Protecting, outlines how to scale and take your real estate career to the next level. Finally, the fifth part, A Success Mindset, walks you through the psychological and emotional mindsets that can either derail or jump-start your real estate career.

Throughout the book, I will share stories and examples of the various principles in action. Some of these are real-world examples (with names and some details changed to protect individuals' identities), and others are fictional anecdotes based on the patterns that I've seen time and time again. I've also included several of my own experiences—both the successes and the mistakes—so that you can learn from my lessons and get a head start on your own path to freedom.

At the end of each chapter, I've included a Take Action Exercise to help you reflect on what you've learned, so you can begin putting it into action. Printable versions of these exercises are available at www.lambertbonus.com.

Finally, the focus of this book is creative financing, short- and long-term rentals, and fix and flips, but most of the principles included here would apply to other types of real estate deals as well, such as multifamily real estate or commercial real estate.

With this book, I want to set you firmly on the path to passive income and an active life—the kind of financial independence that lets you do what you want, when you want, with whom you want, and for how long you want. So let's get started!

PART I

VISION AND STRATEGY

CHAPTER 1

DESIGN YOUR FINANCIAL INDEPENDENCE JOURNEY

Conner loved his job as an engineer and didn't want to quit, but he wanted an extra stream of income to live his dreams. He decided to jump into real estate part time. He was consistent, constantly putting in ten hours every single week. He first purchased a triplex and rented it out for three years before selling it for a huge profit. He continued adding a couple houses to his portfolio every year, flipping some and renting others until he slowly accumulated a massive cash flow. He never quit his job, but he reduced his hours so he'd have more time to pursue his dreams.

Allan pursued a career in Hollywood, but after several years without a breakthrough, he realized it just wasn't going to happen. He became a realtor, but got tired of having to be the servant of every client that he acquired. When he saw the potential of real estate investing, he decided to go all in and do it full time. He was especially attracted to flipping houses and loved to find and manage the deal. He'd flip as many as fifteen to twenty homes a year, and he made great money. Without a job to hold him down, he was able to travel around the world for weeks at a time with his family.

These are two separate paths of real individuals on my real estate investing team. Some people choose to invest part time as a side career, and some go all in and quit their regular jobs. No real estate career looks exactly the same, and the path you choose will depend on your personal goals. But no matter what path you want to take, there are some universal keys for success to follow when getting started. In this chapter, I'll take you through those keys for success. I'll also detail my own journey into real estate investing, with an emphasis on missteps, so that you can have a smoother start into your own real estate career.

KEYS FOR SUCCESS

When I was still a professor, distracting myself from my dissatisfaction by working in my garden, I began reading and listening to all the books I could find about becoming wealthy. From all those books about super successful individuals, I realized that there were a certain set of steps to starting any new career, including real estate: become educated, then get a mentor, and lastly, find a community of like-minded individuals to collaborate with.

GET EDUCATED

To become a successful professor, I had to go to dozens of classes and learn the content I would be teaching to my students. About every serious career requires years of education and training to do it right. Becoming a successful real estate investor is no different. Most of the horror stories you've heard of people making bad investments and losing big in real estate are because they didn't know what they didn't know.

Many people think they can learn everything they need in real estate by listening to some podcasts or by watching YouTube videos. I like to ask people, "Would you hire an accountant to do your taxes who learned everything about his profession by surfing the internet? Would you trust a doctor to operate on your heart who learned how by watching other doctors perform surgeries on YouTube?" Not me!

When I began my career in real estate investment, I knew that, to do it right, I would have to get some formal education. I highly recommend you do the same. But be sure to do your research, because there are also some unhelpful, borderline-scam programs out there, as you'll see in my own journey, detailed later in the chapter. If you reach out to me via www.lambertbonus.com, I can share my most up-to-date recommendations for quality education programs.

GET MENTORSHIP

I decided, as a graduate student, that I wanted to become a highly successful professor. I knew publication was the most important currency to attain academic success, so I sought out someone who was publishing like crazy and who had trained many students to achieve similar success. I knew having a mentor who was publishing in the best psychology journals in the field was my ticket to the big leagues. I found that mentor in Frank, a publishing machine from Florida State University. We shared a lot of common research interests, and he was willing to take me on. Frank pushed me hard and showed me the systems to publish like crazy. It was through his mentorship and help that I was able to become a highly regarded professor. He helped set my sights high and took the time to really show me the ropes.

Mentorship is important in every field, not just academia, and finding a real estate mentor is key to getting where you want to go. Quality mentorship can be hard to find, though.

You are going to want someone who has a great deal of experience in many deals, but who also has the time and motivation to help you. Realistically, the investors doing a lot of deals don't have time for one-on-one mentoring. But you can get the same or similar benefit of mentorship in a small-group setting. You can get regular individual attention and a chance to go over deals and ask questions. The small-group setting is perfect, because you can mastermind and synergize with other people in the group. You can do deals with them and learn from their questions and experiences as well.

FIND A COMMUNITY OF COLLABORATORS

I am a committed Christian, and my faith community is a vital part of who I am. Surrounding myself with people who share my beliefs and support my faith is a vital ingredient for my spiritual thriving and success. It's no different when starting a new career investing in real estate: you need a community of collaborators.

It is vital to surround yourself with entrepreneurs who are on the same path as you are. There have been countless times when I became discouraged on my journey and ran into roadblocks. I needed to run things by someone else who understood. A good community can give you people to run ideas by as well as providing moral support, which is crucial for continued persistent action. If you attempt to go it alone, you will very likely give up. Plus, a good community can help you find people for your dream real estate team (which is discussed in more detail in chapter 14).

Local real estate investing clubs can be a good start, but meetings are usually infrequent, and different people come every time, so it's challenging to build lasting relationships. I've been so blessed to be a part of a massive, nationwide community. This has been a game changer for me, and finding something like this could make all the difference for you as well. Again, I'm happy to provide some up-to-date recommendations for outstanding real estate communities if you reach out.

MY PATH FROM POOR PROFESSOR TO ROCKING REAL ESTATE TYCOON

Knowing I needed education, mentorship, and a community to be successful, I embarked on a journey to find my path to real estate investment. I didn't transform from poor professor to rocking real estate tycoon overnight. It took time—and several missteps—to find my way.

FINDER COMPANY FAIL

My first attempt to become educated and get some help came from a finder company that rehabs properties in good areas for cash flow and sells them to investors as rentals. I joined this company while still working as a professor. They gave me a few videos that helped me learn some of the core essentials of real estate investing. They identified an out-of-state property that would provide me with a monthly cash flow. I was able to get a home equity line of credit on my house and used that for the down payment on this other house. It worked, and I got my first deal!

The downside was the $38,000 down payment used up all the equity in my credit line. I wanted to keep doing more real estate investing, but with my paycheck-to-paycheck situation, I would be unable to buy another property for decades. So my first deal was both a success and a fail. Essentially, I'd won a battle, but I wasn't getting closer to winning the war. What could I do to quench my thirst for real estate wealth? How could I continue?

GURU CIRCUS

I heard there were different, creative ways to find deals. One idea I was curious about was seller financing. I was very excited about the prospect of using other people's money and other people's credit to continue investing, as I was out of both. I learned that a famous real estate investor was going to be doing a workshop in my area, and I couldn't wait to take part.

Upon arrival at the workshop, I felt disappointment. The

famous investor wasn't there himself. I was intrigued enough that I decided to pay $300 to attend the three-day boot camp. The boot camp was a sales pitch for some expensive investing programs. However, because they taught me some true principles, I believed they were going to be there for me. I decided to sign up for their expensive program. It was a mistake. Companies like this paint an enchanting destination in your mind but give no detail about how to get there. As a result, most participants never reach it. It's nothing more than a compelling mirage.

For example, I attended this particular company's advanced course on probate, and I got excited to take action. I went to the county records' building and got some names of people who were on probate and began reaching out to them. It got discouraging fast, as I didn't know what to say to these people on the phone or even what I could offer them on their property. The 1-800 "support" line from the guru company was not at all helpful, and their online community support they had pitched was a total joke.

I began calling this company and *so* many others like it "the guru circus." Just like the circus, these groups come to town, give a good show for a few days, and then roll out of town. They provide no help or support. Like so many others, I was left completely alone to try and figure it out on my own.

REALTOR LICENSE HOUSE FAIL

It was around this point in my journey when I reached the crossroads in my career. I had to decide whether to fight for my job or take a leap of faith into the unknown. I didn't exactly have a track record in real estate yet, as my first two attempts to get educated, find a mentor, and find a community had mostly ended in failure. Yet I could not give up on this dream. I knew I would always regret it if I didn't dedicate my full efforts to real estate, so I quit my job as a professor.

Now I was no longer locked into my current college-town location, and I recognized my house had gone up in value. If I could finish the basement, get my realtor license, and sell the house, I could make a lot of money. This could set me up for more deals. The problem was that I had a fixed income and had already tapped out my equity. I had to get creative. I invited some students to live in my basement and in some of the other bedrooms in my house for free in exchange for their labor. At one point, I had six students living and working in my house and preparing it for sale. I worked alongside them as I listened to my 120 hours of coursework to get my realtor license.

Unfortunately, this approach was taking forever. I got a loan on my 401(k) and maxed out my credit cards so I could hire a contractor to finish the job. I had just enough to finish everything up and put the house on the market.

But the house didn't sell.

The house had a very steep driveway. Every time someone came to look at it, their car would scrape on the way out, nullifying any good feelings they had about the house. Indeed, no offers came in. It was now October, and the upcoming snow would only further exacerbate the problem of the driveway. I was starting to wonder if I had made a terrible mistake in switching careers. What had I done to my young family? Would I have to go bankrupt and move in with my mom just to survive? To make matters even worse, as I was driving to a real estate meeting, my engine went out, and I didn't have any money to replace it. I had to beg my older brother to let me use his extra car until my house sold. My wife was getting nervous and depressed, and I was losing hope. I was thinking seriously about giving up.

THE FULL PACKAGE

Someone invited me to a meeting with a real estate community, and I decided to give it a try. I nearly walked out when I heard it was another paid program, as I'd already spent so much money without getting the results I was promised. Yet something kept me there. I listened and saw there was a large community of people who seemed very willing to share ideas and help me out. I was getting mentorship, and the classes were phenomenal. I was getting everything I needed: education, mentorship, and a support community.

This trifecta isn't easy to find, but it is crucial for ultimate success.

One important principle I learned in this new group was about selling my house *Subject To* my existing mortgage. This simply meant that I would stay on the mortgage, but open up the opportunity for someone who, for whatever reason, couldn't qualify for a bank loan. I would be the bank and create my own financing terms with the buyer. This one little trick changed everything. When I began advertising that I was willing to be the bank, I got two offers right away, and this further maximized the profit.

MY NEWFOUND FREEDOM

I will never forget the relief I felt the day we closed on that house. I drove to a special place in the mountains and, with tears of gratitude, thanked God in prayer. I had put everything on the line for this and was afraid of losing everything. In a single transaction, I had received a check for $109,000, nearly double my annual professor salary. I knew at that moment I had made the right decision, and I would be a real estate investor for the rest of my life.

My wife and I had a favorite TV show, *House Hunters International*. We dreamed of one day having the experience of living abroad. Since we had already sold our house and made all this money, we figured we'd sell everything else and live our dream and move to Fiji for seven months! It was an experience of a lifetime. While there, we auditioned and got the chance to star on an episode of *House Hunters International*. Choosing to get into real estate investing has allowed us to live our dreams, and it has helped us create new dreams.

When we came back, I got to work. With the proper education and mentorship, I did one deal after another after another until I felt like I had nailed it. Then, with the support of so many wonderful people in this community, I began to scale my investing and do as many as fourteen flips at a time.

I was able to purchase my dream car, a Tesla Model S, and I love the self-driving mode! Then, at the end of 2019, we bought our dream house, a nine-thousand-square-foot mansion in the foothills of the mountains. It's equipped with three kitchens, a game room, a sports court, a massive theater room, a huge yard, and everything we could have wanted.

Freedom for me is more than being able to buy the things I want; it's having the time and flexibility to travel and explore various cultures. So as I scaled my investing, I created systems and became less and less involved in each deal until I had more freedom over my time. Soon I was able to spend much of the year traveling while still making more money than ever before! Thus, my Financial Independence Tour was born.

MY FINANCIAL INDEPENDENCE TOUR

For me, freedom means having the money to buy plane tickets and amazing accommodations, while also having the time and schedule flexibility to explore the globe. Here's what my Financial Independence Tour looked like in 2019. As a family, we spent three months on vacation, visited thirteen countries, took forty-seven flights, and lived in forty-nine residences.

- December and January—Thailand, Cambodia, Laos, and Burma for three and a half weeks
- February—Southern Florida for ten days
- April—England and Scotland for eight days
- June and July—Russia, Greece, and Republic of Georgia for four weeks
- August—Panama for eight days
- October—Hawaii for eleven days
- December and January—China, India, and Maldives for three weeks

This list doesn't include short trips to local areas like Lake Powell, Bear Lake (twice), and East Canyon (twice).

My family and I experienced many priceless benefits from our travels:

- *Memories*. We've made enough memories to last a lifetime! The boys are constantly reminiscing and looking at pictures from these trips! These memories are worth more than any physical possession I have.
- *Family relationships*. I am so fortunate to spend almost every waking moment with my best friend and wife, Olya! I get to spend so much time interacting with each of my boys on these trips, and they are hanging out with each other instead of with friends. This creates incredible family unity!
- *Learning time*. I don't zone out on these trips but am intentional about using the time for family and personal development. On the Thailand/Cambodia trip, for instance, Olya and I immersed ourselves in the book *A House United: Changing Children's Hearts and Behaviors by Teaching Self-Government* and began so many new parenting initiatives. Between Russia and Greece I listened to more than twelve audiobooks about mental and physical health. While in India, Olya and I read other earth-shattering parenting books. As we leave the routines of daily life, we experience countless breakthroughs!
- *Broadening cultural horizons*. Every time we go to a new country, we're deepening our understanding of humanity. My children are not only learning history and

geography but seeing how people live and what they value. What a thrill to be so enriched.

- *Motivation.* I put pictures of future destinations on my vision board, and it inspires me to take action like nothing else. I often spend over fifty hours planning a major trip. The planning and anticipation are almost as exciting as the trip itself! Choosing hotels and activities makes this dream very vivid for me. I experience so many aspects of the trip in my mind in advance that it stokes my motivation to make more money, and it provides many hours of sheer joy. Planning a trip has become my favorite way to get into a peak state, which is when you feel energized, focused, and ready to conquer the world.

- *Connection.* When I meet people from different regions of the world, I feel an automatic connection with them. Being well traveled helps me to establish rapport with people immediately. This has helped me tremendously in business. It's also an instant connection with other travelers when you have been to the places they have been.

- *Contribution.* In Cambodia, we contributed the funds to build dozens of wells. These provide clean water to several thousand Cambodian people. We paid to have a school built for Cambodian people to learn English, which gave them a huge leg up in life. It is so meaningful to have my children get involved in helping children in a developing country who so desperately need it.

These are just some of the benefits that financial independence provides me, and I want to help you get to the point where you, too, can be your own boss and be in full control of your time, income, and cash flow.

KEY TAKEAWAYS

To become a successful real estate investor, you need to go on a journey to find education, mentorship, and community, as I did. There's no one right journey, but for a less arduous and turbulent one than mine, learn from my mistakes. Don't rely on finder companies alone, don't fall for the guru circus, and don't try to go it alone.

To succeed, it's also important to establish a compelling vision of what financial independence looks like for you. Make this vision crystal clear. If you skip this step, you will be wandering around without knowing your desired destination. This vision will also serve as a powerful motivational tool. Gaining clarity and understanding around what you are really working toward will bolster you when things get challenging or when you feel like giving up.

The way I define financial independence is being able to do what you want, when you want, with whom you want, and for how long you want. This looks different for every individual. To help create a vivid picture of what financial independence means for you, complete the Take Action

Exercise at the end of this chapter to decide what you want to be, have, and experience when you reach financial independence.

After you complete this exercise, in the next chapter, we'll look at how you can begin building a roadmap to reach this vision, utilizing one of the most foundational beliefs behind freedom real estate investing: prioritizing cash flow over becoming debt-free.

TAKE ACTION EXERCISE:
WHAT DOES FINANCIAL INDEPENDENCE
LOOK LIKE FOR YOU?

*(Download a printable version at
www.lambertbonus.com.)*

Everyone has unique passions and an individual path, so it's important to get clear about what exactly financial independence would look like for you. I want you to create such a compelling future that you are willing to do anything that's legal, moral, and ethical to make it happen. The way I define financial independence is being able to do what you want, when you want, with whom you want, for how long you want. Imagining you have complete financial independence, answer the following questions, divided into three categories: have, be, and experience.

HAVE

What physical possessions would you have?

What car would you be driving?

What house would you be living in?

What products would you be using to enhance your life?

What toys would you buy?

What else would you want to have in your life?

BE

Whom could you become with more time freedom?

Whom would you spend more time with?

What hobbies would you take up?

What passions would you pursue?

What area of your life would you work on to take to the next level? Whom would you hire (like a personal trainer or coach) to take you there?

How would you give back (for example, would you like to be a philanthropist digging wells for people in Third World countries, someone helping others to overcome addictions)?

EXPERIENCE

Where would you travel?

What cultures or ethnic foods would you experience?

What unique experiences would you try (for example, skydiving, hang gliding, scuba diving, doors-off helicoptering, parasailing)?

What shows, concerts, etc., would you see?

What famous people would you like to meet and have lunch with?

CHAPTER 2

FOCUS ON BUILDING CASH FLOW, NOT BECOMING DEBT-FREE

At thirty-five years old, Jim had a goal to become debt-free by paying off his student loans, his car, and his house. He loved Dave Ramsey and learned that you should never go into debt for anything besides a house and that you should pay that debt off as soon as possible. Jim was already living paycheck to paycheck, but every month he was able to make his house payment. It seemed like it was taking forever, though, and when Jim looked at his statement breakdown, most of his payment was going to interest. Jim finally paid off his student loan and his car, but by then his expenses had increased, and he couldn't seem to put anything extra into paying off his house.

Finally, after many years, Jim met his lifelong goal of paying off his house. His timing couldn't have been better because it came a week before he retired. Great time to no longer have a house payment and to finally be debt-free! Jim always wanted to travel the world in retirement, but now that retirement has arrived, he realizes his finances and health won't allow it. Although he doesn't have to make the mortgage payment, his taxes are higher than he thought, and he still has to pay insurance. Also, his pension turned out to be smaller than he had expected. Without his monthly salary coming in, he ends up having to take a loan on his house so that he can make ends meet. Things didn't turn out at all the way he thought they would.

In contrast, Sarah, also thirty-five years old, wanted a fantastic lifestyle. She didn't want to wait until retirement to live her life. She wondered how she'd be able to enjoy life now while also having money saved up for her retirement later. She decided to get more debt now, while she's young, in order to invest in rental properties, and then she could have her tenants pay the debt off for her. Her calculations suggested that if she wanted $15,000 a month to live on in retirement, she would need to buy fifteen rental properties. Once she hit that magic number, she could then work on becoming debt-free. She tapped into the equity in her home and her retirement accounts, and worked with money partners to buy properties. Within a few years, she had reached her goal of fifteen properties. After expenses, she was netting about $6,000 extra per month, which she used to supplement her salary.

Sarah didn't want to wait to see the world with her family, and used the cash flow to start living her dream now. She then began paying off these loans quickly using both her tenants' payments and credit lines (see chapter 3). By the time she was fifty, she had managed to pay off all the mortgages. Now she was making $15,000 a month from her rentals and no longer needed her salary. She retired early. Although she now enjoys being debt-free, she has access to $5 million in low-interest credit lines and can borrow against her properties, tax-free, to do whatever she wants, whenever she wants.

Tell me this: do you want to be like Jim or like Sarah?

Jim and Sarah experienced vastly different outcomes due to one fundamental difference in belief: Jim prioritized becoming debt-free, while Sarah focused on building her monthly cash flow. This is a key lesson to learn in real estate investing—work to reach your financial independence number of rental properties before seeking to become debt-free.

THE IDIOCY OF BECOMING DEBT-FREE

If you asked people about their first-priority financial goal, the vast majority—I'd say as much as 98 percent—would say to become debt-free. However, it's all but impossible to become financially independent without debt, because all assets are tied to debt in the beginning. As a result, having a mindset of avoiding debt is one of the biggest barriers new real estate investors face.

Debt gets a bad rap in our society and for good reason. Consumer debt and interest payments suck the life out of most Americans from the time they graduate from college onward. Everyone wants to get out of that terrible debt treadmill that feels like it will never end.

The problem with becoming debt-free is, while your monthly expenses go down, you still have many fixed expenses. These include things like food, gasoline, insurance, and taxes that need to be paid every month regardless of becoming debt-free. Essentially, being debt-free does not *produce* any income, it only *reduces your expenses*.

It's important to understand that there's good debt and bad debt. Good debt puts money in your pocket at the end of every month, and bad debt takes money out of your pocket. For instance, say you buy a motor home with a credit card. It might provide fun memories for your family, but it doesn't provide any income, and you have to pay for it every month.

That's bad debt. However, you could turn this into good debt simply by renting out the motor home to others whenever you aren't using it yourself. Suddenly, this liability that was taking money away from you each month is now generating income for you. I actually did this!

I agree you should reduce your bad debt—like consumer debt for liabilities such as a boat or a fancy car—at least until you have enough income-producing assets to make the payments for you. But good debt—investing your money in income-producing assets, like a rental property that can churn out monthly payments called cash flow—is your key to financial independence.

IT'S ALL ABOUT CASH FLOW

Your goal should be to find ways to purchase more income-producing assets that generate cash flow. Cash flow is the money left over from rental income generated by a property after paying all the expenses of the property (for example, mortgage, utilities, taxes, insurance, property management fees, and maintenance). You can use that cash flow to pay off your business debt faster, buy more properties, or make the payments on the fun things in life, like a motor home or a dream car, like I did.

Having cash-flowing properties is so important because it's the ultimate way to have other people pay off your debt for you. For example, you might be terrified to amass $1 million in property debt. However, imagine having renters who pay down this debt for you a little at a time every month. Over time, having this debt paid off by your renters could make you a millionaire! Not only are they paying down your debt for you, but they are giving you monthly income that you didn't have to do much work for. That's why it's called "passive income," because you did some work to buy and fix up the property, but now you are passively getting money each month purely from owning the property. Naturally, nothing will be completely passive, as you may have to call on someone to fix something every once in a while, but it will be a fraction of the time and effort of a traditional job.

Although rentals are what will provide financial independence for you, you're likely going to need sources of quick cash to fund your rentals. Flips are a great solution to get you this cash! Thus, most of my suggestions throughout the book will also incorporate fix and flips. But the foundation of your strategy should be rental properties. One of your first steps is to determine the number of properties you need to create your desired level of cash flow.

HOW MANY PROPERTIES DO YOU NEED FOR YOUR FINANCIAL INDEPENDENCE GOAL?

In the chapter 1 exercise, you established a clear vision of your dream financial independence goal (if you have not done this exercise yet, please do so now). Your next step is to figure out how many properties you need to get there.

Start by estimating the monthly cash flow you need to live your dream life. Do this by estimating what your monthly expenses will be. Note that these are not your current monthly expenses, but the projected monthly expenses of your dream life.

Then jump onto a website such as Rentometer and check out rentals in your area, examining what properties are being rented for. I suggest focusing on the entry level to midrange homes, as the upper-income houses probably won't produce a cash flow. The mortgages on larger houses are so high that your monthly payments will typically cost more than what people are willing to pay in rent. Plus, there's simply not enough demand for these large houses because few can afford them.

Next, use a website such as Redfin to determine the approximate annual taxes and divide by twelve to get your monthly tax payment. Make sure to get an estimate for the insurance payment as well. Then, take the monthly rent and subtract the monthly tax and insurance payment.

Finally, factor in that you will be paying approximately 10 percent for a property manager, 10 percent for vacancies, and 10 percent for maintenance and repairs. Take the gross rent number you got from Rentometer and multiply it by 0.3. Subtract this amount as well, and this will give you an approximate estimate of what a paid-off property will yield in cash flow per month.

Here's an example. In my area, the average rent is about $1,800. Now let's say $300 of that goes to taxes and insurance, so that leaves me with $1,500. Now I multiply the $1,800 by 0.3 to account for the other costs, which equals $540. I subtract that from $1,500, and that gives me about $960 in cash flow per property per month.

Now, to determine how many rentals you need to achieve your dreams, divide your desired monthly cash flow goal by the average monthly cash flow for rental properties in your area. Let's say my goal was to get $15,000 coming in passively per month. I would divide 15,000 by 960 to determine how many rentals I would need to hit that income goal. In this case, I would need to own about fifteen or sixteen rentals free and clear to receive $15,000 per month. You'll have a chance to run your own numbers in the Take Action Exercise at the end of the chapter.

KEY TAKEAWAYS

The most common financial goal of most Americans is to get out of debt. However, they try to get out of debt before they have acquired assets. This is a mistake. Instead, figure out how much passive income you need for financial independence. Then pile on all kinds of income-producing debt until you have acquired enough rentals to reach the passive income you desire. The Take Action Exercise at the end of this chapter will help you estimate how many properties you will need to reach your desired amount of passive income.

Once you've achieved your passive-income goal, it makes all the sense in the world to become debt-free! *Alert, alert,* the ultimate paradigm shift to show you how to get rid of this debt *fast* is coming in the next chapter! With a strategy I call the Debt Paydown Accelerator, you will see how you can pay off a thirty-year mortgage in five to ten years! Get ready to change your life!

**TAKE ACTION EXERCISE:
HOW MANY PROPERTIES DO YOU
NEED TO REACH YOUR FINANCIAL
INDEPENDENCE GOAL?**

*(Download a printable version at
www.lambertbonus.com.)*

1. Write about one or two things you found most helpful in this chapter that you want to apply to your career.

2. How much passive income do you want monthly for financial independence?

3. What's the average rent in your target area?

4. How many rentals do you need to get to financial Independence?

CHAPTER 3

THE SECRET BANKS DON'T WANT YOU TO KNOW

Sue bought a house with her husband when they got married and was kind of shocked by the percentage that was going to the bank in interest payments. Yet she put it behind her, grateful to have her first house. Five years later, the interest rates dipped. Her favorite mortgage broker approached her to let her know she could decrease her payment by $150 a month if she would refinance. That sounded pretty awesome, so she did. Four years after that, she and her husband got divorced and she moved to a new house. Six years after that, a recession hit, and the same mortgage broker pointed out how interest rates had never been this low. She could reduce her monthly payment by

$120 through refinancing, so she did it. Three years later, she remarried and moved into a bigger, nicer house with her new husband. Five years later, they needed a little money for his business and decided to refinance the new house. Seven years later, their kids had grown up and her knees were getting bad, so Sue and her new husband sold their house and moved into a smaller rambler. Thirty years had now passed, and Sue looked at what percentage of her payment was going to the bank. It dawned on her that for all these years, between 60 percent and 80 percent of her monthly payment had been going to the bank, and she had almost no equity in her home.

At the same time, Rick bought a house with his wife at 4 percent interest. He thought it was a great deal until he noticed what percentage of his payment was going toward interest—around 80 percent. He did some research and realized the bank was counting on most people to sell or refinance every five to seven years. Ultimately, the bank collected a higher percentage on their loan than the most aggressive payday loans. Nobody talks about it, and they are getting away with it! Rick also learned a credit line charges simple daily interest and can be used to avoid this amortization trap the bank sets. He soon refinanced his mortgage into a first-position home equity line of credit (HELOC) and began paying the principal down with his surplus. Five years later, when interest rates dropped, his payments went down even more without him changing anything, since his HELOC was a variable rate and therefore followed national interest rates. This allowed him to pay the house down even faster.

Four years later, he had paid off the entire house, and when he got divorced, he was able to write a check to his ex-wife for her share. He kept the house as a rental when he moved to a new house, which he purchased with a first-position HELOC. He used the rest of his equity to make down payments on five other properties, all with HELOCS. Six years later, a recession hit, and his interest rate on all seven of his houses went down. He used the equity from all his houses and put down payments on eight other houses, bringing his total to fifteen houses. Three years later, he remarried and moved with his new wife into a bigger and nicer house, which was purchased with a HELOC. Five years later, when he needed money for his business, he funded it with a check from his HELOC. Seven years after that, their kids had grown, so Rick moved into his favorite rambler rental and turned his big house into a short-term rental on Airbnb. The same thirty years had now passed, and Rick had successfully acquired fifteen properties *and* paid them all off. Furthermore, he had paid a tiny fraction per house of the interest Sue had paid in the same time period.

Although their life circumstances were roughly equal, who would you want to trade places with, Sue or Rick? My aim in this chapter is to show you how amortized loans crush you with unending high interest and no flexibility. The secret that the banks don't want you to know is that they charge the average person over 60 percent interest but that you can avoid this by using credit lines. Using credit lines as your new checking account will save you millions in interest while giving you unlimited flexibility. This fundamental understanding will be key to your success as a real estate investor.

THE PROBLEM WITH AMORTIZED LOANS

Right before buying my first house, I'll never forget scratching my head and wondering how the bank makes any money by charging me a measly 4 percent interest. "Wow, they are so generous; that's so nice of them," I naively thought. I wondered what the catch was and whether the government subsidized them so they could give such great rates. I will also never forget the horror I experienced as I looked at how much of my payment (nearly 80 percent) was going to the bank compared to paying down the principal. I was horrified to see how it was going to take over sixteen years before more than half of my payment went to pay down the principal.

It now dawned on me that the bank can say 4 percent, because if you hold the loan for the full thirty years, then your average interest rate is 4 percent. However, they take most of their interest up front. They know only a tiny fraction of homeowners will make it all the way through without ever moving or refinancing.

A mortgage is called an "amortized" loan. This means the loan is calculated using a complicated mathematical formula to lower your monthly payment. This sounds great at first, but be aware, banks don't do it out of kindness. Banks know that, on average, people refinance after seven years. This starts the clock and the 80 percent interest all over.

Not as good of a deal as it sounded, is it? Let me illustrate. Let's pretend we bought a home with a small down payment. Here are the important parts:

Loan amount: $300,000
Interest: 5 percent
Monthly payment: $1,625.13

Not bad, at first glance, anyway.

Here is where the banks get tricky!

Your first payment: $1,625.13
Interest: $1,291.67
Principal: $333.46
True starting interest rate: 79.48 percent

Now that is *not* what most people signed up for! If you don't believe me, look at your statement!

Remember, we agreed to a 5 percent interest rate, not to 79.48 percent.

The sneaky truth is you'll have to have the same loan for the *entire* thirty years to actually get the 5 percent interest rate you agreed to!

You may be thinking, well, yeah, but the interest part goes down over time. You would be right, but it doesn't go down very quickly. At the end of the first year, you will still average a 77.47 percent interest rate!

AMORTIZED LOAN SCHEDULE

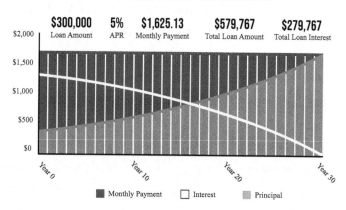

$300,000	5%	$1,625.13	$579,767	$279,767
Loan Amount	APR	Monthly Payment	Total Loan Amount	Total Loan Interest

Monthly Payment   Interest   Principal

FIRST PAYMENT BREAKDOWN

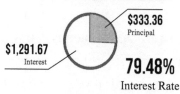

$333.36
Principal

$1,291.67
Interest

79.48%
Interest Rate

That's right...the first several years you're making payments on your mortgage, you'll be paying an astronomical amount of interest. That is way worse than any credit card I've *ever* seen, no matter how bad your credit may be!

LOANS VERSUS LINES

You may not have even realized there was a difference between the two, but a loan and a line of credit work completely differently. Most people are familiar with how a bank loan, such as a mortgage, works. Yet many are completely unfamiliar with how different a line of credit is in interest, monthly payment, and flexibility. The stark differences may shock you, and you'll be scratching your head wondering why anyone would ever sign up for a loan.

INTEREST

Approximately 70 to 80 percent of your payment in a loan is going to interest for the first several years. After that, it declines until, by month 359, you're paying almost nothing in interest, and it averages out to what they tell you on paper. The problem is that almost nobody makes it that far, so most people end up paying 60 to 80 percent in interest.

Conversely, a line of credit charges simple daily interest, so you're paying interest only on what you're using on a particular day. That means if you charged your credit line

$10,000 and then paid it off three days later, you would only be charged interest on the $10,000 for the three days you were using it. Most home equity credit lines are around 5 percent interest, which is *way* better than 60 to 80 percent. Even if you use a credit card at 21 percent, that is still three to four times cheaper than an amortized mortgage you hold for five to seven years.

MONTHLY PAYMENT

Another huge problem with a loan is that the payment stays the same regardless of the balance. So, let's say you have a $20,000 loan and you made $15,000 in a lump sum from flipping a house. You pay that on the loan. Your payment doesn't change at all.

Conversely, if that $20,000 balance were a credit line and you paid it down $15,000, your monthly payment would decrease by 75 percent! You could use the extra money that was not required for the payment to pay down your line much faster. It's like a snowball where you can pay it down faster and faster the further down the "hill" you get!

FLEXIBILITY

Another huge problem with a loan is that it provides no flexibility. For instance, let's say you're at the car wash with your new Tesla and some uninsured motorist rams into you.

It causes thousands of dollars of damage with no recourse. This happened to me! If you put all your monthly surplus into your loan and then ask the bank to give you back $2,000 to fix your Tesla, what are they going to tell you? First of all, they wouldn't understand what you were asking. If they did, they would tell you to "take a hike." Nobody is going to aggressively pay down a loan with all their surplus because then they would have nothing left for these kinds of emergencies.

Conversely, when you have a line of credit, you can put every penny of your monthly income into paying it down, since you can pull it out at any time if you need it! For instance, I pulled $2,000 out of my line of credit to fix my Tesla and continued to put all my income into the credit line to pay it back down. I know I have access to the money whenever I need it. That makes me feel confident about using every dime of my income to pay down my debt. In fact, there was a time when I sold a bunch of flips, and in four months, I paid $400,000 down on my credit lines using this method!

This flexibility can be a disadvantage if you are not fiscally responsible, as you could end up never paying your house off. So do pay attention to how you're using your credit line, and make sure you're making progress in paying your house off.

HOW TO BEAT THE BANKS AT THEIR OWN GAME: THE DEBT PAYDOWN ACCELERATOR

Okay, now that the complicated stuff is out of the way, let's talk about how you can beat the banks at their own game with the Debt Paydown Accelerator. I'll show you four easy steps that could save you hundreds of thousands of dollars in interest over time.

Remember, we started out with a $300,000 mortgage. This is what you do next:

1. Pay off the mortgage with a simple-interest home equity line at, say, 5 percent interest (keep in mind that HELOCs usually have a variable rate, meaning that the rates can fluctuate with the national interest rate). Find a HELOC with a high loan-to-value ratio of 85 to 100 percent so you can have access to as much of your equity as possible. In other words, find a bank that will let you tap as much of your equity as possible.

2. Turn your HELOC into your banking account and deposit all your income at the beginning of the month into your HELOC. This will keep the balance on your HELOC interest rate as low as possible. You're paying simple daily interest, so if you can have a lower balance for a big part of the month, you'll save a great deal on interest.

3. Use your HELOC to pay your monthly expenses. You can do this with a checkbook or a debit card that is

directly connected to your HELOC. You can pay for groceries, gas, anything with your HELOC! Allow any surplus to remain in the account to eventually pay your HELOC balance down to zero. Note that this strategy does not work if you're living paycheck to paycheck. For example, if your expenses exceed your monthly income, then you will never pay off your debt. You need at least some surplus at the end of every month, even just fifty dollars, to pay down the principal.

4. When you reach a zero balance, you can use the entire line of credit to do whatever you want. Also, you can use any part of the equity in your home at any time along the way to buy another rental.

Here's a comparison of the HELOC method versus an amortized mortgage:

MORTGAGE PAYDOWN SHOWDOWN

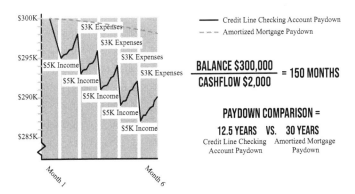

Credit Line Checking Account Paydown
Amortized Mortgage Paydown

$$\frac{\text{BALANCE } \$300,000}{\text{CASHFLOW } \$2,000} = 150 \text{ MONTHS}$$

PAYDOWN COMPARISON =

12.5 YEARS   VS.   30 YEARS
Credit Line Checking   Amortized Mortgage
Account Paydown   Paydown

In the Take Action Exercise at the end of the chapter, I'll take you through the steps of calculating how long it would take you to pay off your mortgage with this approach.

TAKING IT TO THE NEXT LEVEL

This isn't just a trick to pay off your own home. It's also a way to fund other deals and become a millionaire! These credit lines can be such a powerful way to pay off multiple rental properties. I want to open your mind to the possibilities here!

Let's say you have $200,000 of equity in your current home and you switch it into a home equity line of credit. Now, instead of paying off your debt (which I pointed out is a bad goal in the previous chapter), you could take that equity and make ten down payments of $20,000. Let's say each of these rentals provides $400 in monthly cash flow. When you buy ten, you're adding $4,000 to your monthly cash flow. If you already had $3,800 in cash flow, you now have $7,800. The key with many properties is to combine all the cash flow to knock out one mortgage at a time. Now, if the loan on each of these properties were $100,000, your cash flow could pay off a rental in under thirteen months ($100,000/$7,800 = 12.82 months)!

Once that mortgage is paid off, then your cash flow increases by $800, so your new cash flow is $8,600 a month. You can apply that cash flow to paying down the second rental, and it is going to get paid off even faster ($100,000/$8,600 = 11.5 months)! Now you add another $800 to your cash flow, and your new cash flow is $9,400 per month.

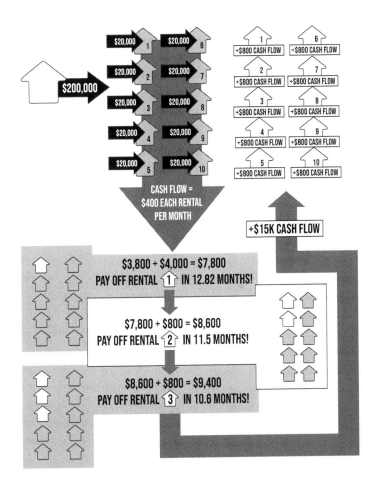

The third rental is again paid off even faster ($100,000/$9,400 = 10.6 months)! So, you see it accelerates faster and faster until you have completely paid off all the rentals and your cash flow hits $15,000 per month. At this point, you will have all kinds of equity, and you will have paid off all your debt, sitting pretty for the rest of your life! This is what is possible with the Debt Paydown Accelerator strategy.

KEY TAKEAWAYS

Mortgages are bad news. We think we're getting 3 to 5 percent interest loans, but in practicality, the banks are charging the average homeowner 60 to 80 percent in interest. To top it off, the banks give no flexibility on monthly payment. They don't allow you to withdraw any money out of the loan without paying for an expensive refinance that starts the interest clock over.

Conversely, lines of credit charge only a simple daily rate for what you are using on any particular day. Your payment shrinks as you pay it down, and you can pull money out at any time, which gives you the possibility of using your entire income to pay off your debt. Use a home equity line of credit as you would a checking account. By attacking your debt with all your income, you could pay off your house in a third of the time without changing your income. Even better, a home equity line of credit allows you to pull money out for down payments on other properties. So get your house pregnant and start having some baby houses today!

In the next chapter, we'll cover the last big, foundational strategic decision you must make to succeed as a real estate investor: becoming a team leader instead of a do-it-yourselfer.

TAKE ACTION EXERCISE:
HOW FAST CAN YOU PAY OFF
YOUR MORTGAGE?

(Download a printable version at
www.lambertbonus.com.)

1. Write about one or two things you found most helpful in this chapter that you want to apply to your career.

2. What is your mortgage balance (or other debt balance)?

3. What is your net income every month?

4. What are your average expenses?

5. What is your monthly cash flow (income minus expenses)?

6. How many months until you can pay off your balance without increasing your income (mortgage balance / monthly cash flow)?

7. What if you flip a house for $24,000 and add $2,000 a month to your cash flow? Now what does your payoff look like? How many months until you pay off your debt? (Hint: mortgage balance / monthly cash flow + $2,000.)

CHAPTER 4

TEAM LEADER VERSUS DO-IT-YOURSELFER

Joe is a very hands-on kind of guy, and when he decided to get into real estate investing, he was excited to use some of his rehabbing skills to save on costs. Not only that, when Joe found a property to flip, he moved his entire family into the house and sold his other house to further save on costs. Joe's wife wasn't too thrilled about this idea to begin with, but when it was time to renovate the kitchen and she lost access to it, she got pretty frustrated. She also lost access to the master bath and had to share a bathroom with three of her children. Everything always took longer than Joe thought it would, especially because he was trying to work his full-time job and get all this done on nights and week-ends. It took a full nine months to get everything finished, and another two months on the selling market. This was seven months longer than it would have taken had Joe hired help. Plus, he and his family had to clean and leave whenever potential buyers came to look at the house. Joe's wife was about ready to file for divorce, she was so frustrated, and Joe's boss actually came pretty close to firing him due to a drop in job performance. Joe was often falling asleep on the job, and for a month he was unable to use his right hand due to a project-related injury.

Still, Joe felt like it was all worth it, since he saved probably $10,000 in labor costs. What Joe didn't take into account were all the payments he was making on the house during the extended time it took to finish. He ended up paying an extra $4,500 to the lender for these extra seven months. He also missed the peak selling season, costing him far more than $10,000 in potential lost revenue. His total profit ended up being $25,000.

* * *

Bob is anything but gifted with his hands. In fact, he usually needs to call on his wife or AAA to change a tire because he doesn't get how to do it. Yet Bob is a very gifted delegator. When Bob acquired his first property to flip, the first thing he did was ask his Facebook friends for contractor referrals. He visited the house with his contractor, and they discussed at length everything he wanted to have completed. Then he let the contractor do his job. He would check in every week and go over the progress with his contractor, but it was the contractor calling most of the shots.

Bob was nervous this project might take up too much time and interfere with his job and his personal life. However, it wasn't bad at all. In fact, Bob was able to spend most of his free time looking for his next deal and purchased two more properties during the three months of renovation. As his first property sat on the market, he got his crew to work on the second property and found another crew to work on the third. In fact, after having found the first three properties on his own, Bob employed some of the young adults in his neighborhood. They knocked on doors that had a notice of default. With these systems in place, Bob was able to buy another two properties to flip, both of which took an extra four to five months to rehab and sell. He had paid his deal finders and construction crews well. As a result, he didn't have as high a margin per deal as he could have. By delegating, he was able to complete five flips in his first eleven months for a total profit of $110,000.

Who would you want to trade places with, Joe or Bob? Yes, Bob made less profit per property than Joe, but he made far more total profit with a lot more time freedom. Time freedom is realized by those who learn to delegate all tasks except those that require true unique ability. If you don't learn to delegate, you will trade one job for another very stressful job. Instead of thinking "How can I do all this?" think "Who can do this?" In this chapter, I hope to change your mindset to one of a team leader, rather than a do-it-yourselfer.

FLIPPING: USE CONTRACTORS!

You would be surprised how many people flip houses like Joe in the previous example. They take control of every aspect of the flip and end up making dozens or even hundreds of trips to their local hardware store and lumber yard. You can't make it in and out of those stores in less than ninety minutes, not to mention all the time spent on the actual repairs. That's a lot of time wasted on something you're probably not even a specialist in. There is so much to learn about finding deals, raising capital, and deal analysis that you don't have time to learn about all the elements of construction and materials.

In the long run, paying a contractor or crew to handle the renovation will save you not only time but often money. Not only can professionals do it better than you, but they can do it much faster than you. This gets you more money in two ways. First, the house will sell for more money because buyers will be able to tell the work was done by a professional. Second, because the work will be completed more quickly, you will pay less in fees to your lender.

You probably want to flip houses to create financial and time freedom in your life, but doing the work yourself will cripple your chances for both. Rather than getting into the weeds on a single deal, focus on finding and funding a higher quantity of deals.

RENTALS: HIRE PROPERTY MANAGERS

This same team-leader mindset applies to rental properties as well. There are a lot of people who hate rental properties. Perhaps you've talked to some of them, or maybe this was your experience. I usually find that the people who hate rentals are the ones who are hands-on. They picked out the tenant themselves and probably did a poor job of screening, so they have an unqualified tenant living in the property. They're fielding the call at midnight with the clogged toilet. They're driving over to collect rent only to find out the tenant isn't at home or has a sob story of why they need an extension. I would hate rentals too, if that were how I did it.

In fact, this is how I used to approach rentals, and I learned my lesson the hard way. I put a listing up myself and the guy sweet-talked me into renting it to him without the proper qualifications. He turned out to be a snake, and I had to evict him. I lost several months' rent and had a nightmare on my hands. I will never make that mistake again.

Now rentals are so easy for me. I only buy properties where

I can get a good enough deal that I can afford to pay a professional to do everything for me. In fact, I haven't met any of my renters, except for the one who lives in the studio apartment of my guest house. I get direct deposits put into my checking account and only hear from my property manager when something big happens—and it rarely does.

If you hire professionals to handle your properties, you'll take away the vast majority of the stress, and you'll be able to scale and get dozens of properties without having to spend much of your time. And time is your most valuable resource.

BUILD SYSTEMS SO YOU CAN ENJOY YOURSELF!

Is McDonald's the most delicious burger on the market? No chance! But they are the largest restaurant franchise in the world and feed approximately 1 percent of the world's population every day. Not only are they not that delicious; they are also run by teenagers. How could this be? They have incredible and proven systems for success.

In real estate, you will first need to figure out how it all works and do a couple of properties. Then you can build systems to scale your business to greater heights, always delegating tasks to your team. For instance, for five years I had my realtor license. I quickly realized that I had gotten to the point where my time was not well spent filling out addresses on contracts and getting things signed. I began hiring other realtors to do all the work for me and, eventually, it didn't seem to make sense to even have my license at all. I decided to let it lapse.

As another example, initially I was finding properties and getting the sellers to sign the contracts. Then I realized I could pay someone else to do this. I never find the properties I flip or rent anymore. I either train someone in my elite mentorship program to find them and partner with me, or I pay a wholesaler for a deal. A wholesaler is someone whose job it is to find real estate deals and then sell the contract to another investor like me. I'm okay with them making some money on the deal, because they saved me the hassle of sending out thousands of mailers, fielding the calls, and negotiating the deal with the seller.

I have systems that find the deal for me. Assistants close the deal for me. Contractor teams rehab the property for me, and realtors sell the property for me. All I need to do is analyze the deal to make sure the numbers work, make a few calls to raise the money, and check in throughout the process with all my teams. I make a bundle of cash doing this every year. This is exactly why I can spend three months on family vacations every year! I can make a few calls and send a few texts to check in on my deals from anywhere in the world, and this can be done in one to two hours per day. Of course, I didn't get to where I am overnight. I had to nail it before I scaled it. In other words, I was more deeply involved in my first couple deals to learn how everything worked. Now I delegate everything to other people to do for me.

KEY TAKEAWAYS

It's a human tendency to try to do everything yourself. Indeed, most of us have been programmed by our parents to save every penny we can through our own efforts. Yet, if you want to have time freedom, you'll need to forget those lessons of the past and learn to delegate everything you can. Don't swing hammers, collect rent, or try to do the paperwork for your own properties. Instead, build teams and systems to do most of the work for you. This will allow you to do what you want, when you want, with whom you want, and for how long you want, and your business won't go under while you're away!

Now that you understand the foundational strategies needed for success, it's time to map out your game plan. In the next chapter, I'll give you ten simple steps to guide you as you start your own real estate investment journey.

TAKE ACTION EXERCISE:
HOW WILL YOU DELEGATE?

(Download a printable version at www.lambertbonus.com.)

1. Write about one or two things you found most helpful in this chapter that you want to apply to your career.

2. What real estate tasks do you feel like you're uniquely qualified for or would love to do yourself (for example, finding the deal, analyzing the deal, making an offer, finding the money, managing the rehab, or marketing the property for sale)?

3. What tasks do you plan to delegate to others in your real estate business?

4. What mental obstacles might you have (if any) that could make you reluctant to delegate to others?

5. What's your plan to overcome these obstacles?

CHAPTER 5

WHAT MY PLAN WOULD BE FOR YOU

Jackson was excited about real estate investing but didn't know where to begin. He spent several months just getting ready to get ready, aimlessly listening to real estate podcasts. He was in love with the idea of investing but was all over the map about where to begin. He finally decided that he was interested in flipping houses, but in a few weeks, he realized it was a lot of work and very costly. Next, he figured he would do short-term rentals. However, once again, he didn't realize how costly and time-consuming it would be to do short-term property management, so he switched again. This time he decided he'd become a wholesaler. He didn't know that he would have to get really good at finding properties and creating a large list of potential buyers to be an effective wholesaler. That wasn't what he had in mind, so he switched strategies again. If that weren't enough, Jackson was similarly all over the board on the strategies he used, switching it up every week or two. He made little time for his attempts, was not consistent, and gave up quickly. Soon, someone showed Jackson how much money he could make in cryptocurrencies. He decided real estate was not for him and moved on to the next shiny object.

Where did Jackson go wrong? He didn't have a good plan. There are so many potential paths to take in real estate and so many things to do, it can truly be overwhelming. You need a game plan, an idea of exactly what steps you need to take to become successful in this most exciting journey. In this chapter, I'll provide you with ten steps to create an action plan that allows you to stay focused on your goals.

#1: SCHEDULE YOURSELF

If you've decided that you want to get on the path to financial independence, scheduling the time to build your business is one of the most important tasks. At the beginning, you will need more time for learning, but after getting over the initial learning curve, I recommend that you spend a minimum of five hours on learning and five hours on taking action each week. Rather than hope that you'll get around to it, be intentional and carve out your learning and action hours on your calendar. Plan what time you will give to this business, and then stick to it no matter what. Naturally, if you put in more than ten hours a week, you will get more results faster. Yet many members of my elite investing team are able to get results with that amount of time, as long as they're consistent.

#2: LEARN THE BASICS

Reading this book is an incredible place to start when it comes to learning the basics of real estate investing. However, you should get additional exposure to some of the basic elements of different types of real estate investing. It's also important to learn more about the mortgage accelerator strategy, taxes, and credit. These topics intersect with real estate and are important for your journey.

#3: DECIDE ON YOUR INVESTING STRATEGY

Once you have explored some of the investing strategies out there, it's time to make a decision on what type of investing you'd like to start out with. Some strategies to consider are long-term rentals, short-term rentals (Airbnb), fix and flip, *Subject To*, or wholesaling. If you do not have much in the way of cash, it may be easier to generate some income with fix and flip or wholesaling. There are so many ways to make money in real estate. Rather than learning about one and doing a deal or two and then shifting to another strategy, like Jackson, it is much better to stay focused. Do a dozen or more properties with the same strategy so that you can become proficient. Then you can add a new strategy to your tool belt and do both simultaneously. The type of investing strategy you decide on will determine the analysis you need to complete as well.

#4: SET YOUR GOALS

Now that you have determined your investing strategy, it's time to determine what goals you have for yourself for the next five to ten years. Consider some of the *be*, *have*, and *experience* items you listed previously in the chapter 1 exercise.

Once you have set your big goals, chunk them down into smaller goals. Start by determining what your goals are for your next twelve months. Will you flip three houses, buy two rentals, get a HELOC on your home, pay off your student loans? Then set the monthly, weekly, and daily goals needed to make this happen. What concrete, specific actions will you need to reach your big goals? You could even track the number of contacts or offers you make. The more specific you can be, the better your results.

#5: MAP OUT YOUR LEARNING PLAN

Your next step will be to gain access to educational material regarding your area of focus. Please don't try to figure it out on your own or think that "internet university" is going to show you how. There's too much that can go wrong in real estate to wing this. Once you have access to quality education, make a plan for which classes you will watch by what target dates. Dive in to really learn about your specialty area of investing. As mentioned previously, ideally, you want to watch or listen to education for at least five hours per week.

#6: PLAN YOUR ACTION FOCUS

Education is vitally important, but if you don't talk to real potential sellers, you will never get a deal or make any money. Don't get ready to get ready; take action today! There are *so* many potential motivated sellers in your market today, but you have to plan which method you will use to communicate with them.

There are five core finding methods: knocking on doors, dialing, mailing, wholesalers, and warm contacts. (See chapter 11 for a breakdown of each of these methods that includes a summary of the pros and cons.) Choose one of these and stick with it for at least three weeks. My elite investor team members and I have had the most success with warm contacts, but you've got to find what you're most comfortable with. Everything works if you work it, but nothing is easy or perfectly ideal.

#7: GAIN ACCESS TO OFF-MARKET DEAL-FINDING SOFTWARE

If you decide to knock on doors, send mailers, or cold-call prospects, you are going to need some software that compiles lists of possible leads. No, you do not want to look for deals on the multiple listing service (MLS). That's where everyone and their dog goes to buy a house, and anything that might have been a deal is almost surely taken already. That is why it's crucial to look for deals that are off market and not listed on the MLS. You can find lists of potentially motivated sellers using software that compiles all the names and addresses of these individuals into one source. These are the people that you want to spend your time reaching out to. Not all of them are going to be interested in selling, but many will, and you can get a sufficient enough discount to make a great profit.

#8: CREATE A SPREADSHEET TO TRACK LEADS

As a realtor, I learned that following up with potential leads is the most important thing you can do. You must have some system for reporting your conversations with different sellers so that you can call them back. Rarely will someone sell you their property with the first conversation. It usually will take repeated connections before they trust you or before they will be motivated enough to sell you their property. Some call their lead-tracking system a customer relationship management (CRM) tool. This could be as simple as a spreadsheet, either on your computer or saved to a cloud spreadsheet program. It should have columns to record the lead's name, address, and phone number, and a notes column where you can write about your interactions with everyone. If you want to get more sophisticated, there are several CRM programs on the market.

#9: CREATE A SPREADSHEET TO TRACK YOUR REAL ESTATE TEAM AND BEGIN RECRUITING

Building a good real estate team is critical, because they will handle most of the elements of the deal for you. I recommend creating a spreadsheet where you track all the real estate professionals that you already know. Then, as you attend networking events or connect with other real estate professionals, add them to your contacts spreadsheet. This can be a great resource for you when you get your first deal under contract. You will already have your contacts lined up and can put them into action. In chapter 14, I will further describe the importance of building your real estate investing team of professionals.

#10: START ANALYZING DEALS AND MAKING OFFERS

As you begin to take action and reach out to sellers, you can start practicing analyzing deals and making offers. In chapter 12, I will give you a lightning analysis strategy that will give you an idea of what you might be able to offer on a property. Then just make the offer! Don't stress out about the seller's response; just treat it in your mind as practice. If the seller accepts your offer, remember that you will have time to do your due diligence and revise your offer if you need to. The important thing is to take action, because you can get out of the offer for any reason later if you need to, something I'll describe more in chapter 19.

KEY TAKEAWAYS

Getting organized and putting your game plan together is crucial for getting into a deal as quickly as possible. Taking action on these ten simple steps will set you up for success—schedule yourself, learn the basics, decide on an investment strategy, set your goals, map out your learning plan, plan your action focus, get access to deal-finding software, create a lead-tracking spreadsheet, create a team-tracking spreadsheet, and then analyze deals and make offers. Following these steps can get you to real estate success in an accelerated fashion.

For additional help and guidance in building your game plan, please visit www.lambertbonus.com, where I provide weekly training, education options, up-to-date software recommendations, and tracker spreadsheet templates—all for free!

TAKE ACTION EXERCISE:
WHAT'S YOUR GAME PLAN?

(Download a printable version at www.lambertbonus.com.)

#1: SCHEDULE YOURSELF

What time during the week will you allot to educating your-self on real estate?

What time during the week will you allot to taking action to find deals?

#2: LEARN THE BASICS

What resource(s) will you use to learn some basics about different real estate strategies?

#3: DECIDE ON YOUR INVESTING STRATEGY

What is your investing strategy (for example, long-term rentals, short-term rentals, flips, wholesale)?

#4: SET YOUR GOALS

List your long-term financial independence goals for five to ten years from now.

List your financial or real estate goals for the next twelve months.

What monthly goals do you need to reach your yearly goals?

What weekly goals do you need to reach your monthly goals?

What daily goals do you need to reach your weekly goals?

#5: MAP OUT YOUR LEARNING PLAN

What resource(s) will you use to gain knowledge about your real estate specialty?

#6: PLAN YOUR ACTION FOCUS

Of the five core deal-finding strategies—knocking on doors, dialing, mailing, wholesalers, and warm contacts (described in depth in chapter 11)—which do you want to use to find deals?

#7: GAIN ACCESS TO OFF-MARKET DEAL-FINDING SOFTWARE

What software or resource will you use to find off-market deals?

#8: CREATE A SPREADSHEET TO TRACK LEADS

Did you create your leads tracker using a Google spreadsheet, Excel, or some other program for your real estate leads?

#9: CREATE A SPREADSHEET TO TRACK YOUR REAL ESTATE TEAM

Did you create your team tracker using a Google spreadsheet, Excel, or some other program to track your real estate team?

#10: START ANALYZING DEALS AND MAKING OFFERS

By what date do you plan to make an offer on a property?

PART II

FINDING THE MONEY

CHAPTER 6

SOURCES OF MONEY

Ebony was convinced that you need several hundred thousand dollars available to you in order to get started with real estate investing. She had a dream to become an investor and so she started saving up to buy a house. She set aside $500 every month pretty consistently. At that pace, to save a minimum of $30,000 for a down payment, it would take her *five years*. That was frustratingly slow, but she stuck with it. Then, a couple years into saving, when she'd saved up $10,000, her daughter had a medical emergency and the cost was $9,000. Now she had to start all over. Her dream of buying several properties felt like it was never going to happen.

No one should have to skimp and save to become a real estate investor. There are all kinds of money sources that await you, including home equity credit lines, retirement accounts, cash value life insurance, personal credit cards, business credit cards, and business credit lines. As we'll see in the following chapters, I recommend using other people's money as much as possible, while using your own money for reserves, but it's important to start with an understanding of all the different sources of money that are available. This will help you gain access to both your own money for reserves and to other people's money for making deals.

HOME EQUITY LINES

Equity sitting in a house is a bit of a waste. It's kind of like having a paid employee sleeping in your attic. Get that equity working and creating more financial independence for you! As stated previously, get your house pregnant and have some baby houses. The great thing about a home equity line of credit is that the interest rate is good when compared to other sources. Also, you are paying only on what you have borrowed at any particular time. This line of credit can be ideal for reserves, since you only pay interest if you have to use it. HELOCs could also be a good source for potential lenders to draw money for deals you do with them.

RETIREMENT ACCOUNTS

Retirement accounts are one of the best possible sources of money. Oftentimes, people have money in their retirement account that is sitting idle and not making them money. Other times, the retirement cash is in a low-interest, under-performing security. There are two ways to use a retirement account.

The first is to get a loan. You can borrow 50 percent, up to $50,000, unless they have changed the rules since this book was published. The interest payments you make go right back into your account. Essentially, you pay yourself interest. Therefore, this is ultimately an interest-free loan.

The second method is better but can typically only be done when a 401(k) is not through a current employer. If it is not, then you can turn that 401(k) into a self-directed 401(k) and invest it in real estate. This can be a powerful way for you to gain access to hundreds of thousands, if not millions, of your own money or others' money. Schedule a call with me through www.lambertbonus.com, and I can show you how to turn your 401(k) into a self-directed account, so you can use 100 percent of it for investing. Also, there are a lot of rules to using this money the right way. It's a bit too much detail for the scope of this book, but if you contact me, I can direct you to this information.

CASH VALUE LIFE INSURANCE

Whole life or indexed universal life insurance policies have what is called a cash value. These policies typically have a way for you to draw a low-interest loan on the cash value and use it for whatever you want. They do charge a low interest rate. Cash value life insurance is a fantastic tool for reserves. You can make money on the interest that's in there. It is very liquid, and you can usually get a loan within a week. You can also receive a death benefit for your family should you die unexpectedly, and thus, it can serve a dual purpose. This is where I store my reserves for my deals.

PERSONAL 0 PERCENT CREDIT CARDS

If you want to avoid having to get a private money lender involved in a deal, you could apply for 0 percent interest cards. I've had a few people give me funds they got from applying for 0 percent interest credit cards. Banks have these promotions you can find on websites such as creditcards.com. You or your money lender can apply for multiple cards at 0 percent interest, which usually lasts twelve to eighteen months. You could use these cards to buy supplies for your fix and flip or to pay your contractors and pay no fees and no interest.

There are also ways to turn the credit cards into cash if needed. Your private money partner could send the money to you through an online payment service for a small transaction fee. Many cards allow for balance transfers, and you can sometimes transfer the money directly to your bank account or write yourself a check for a small fee.

Since the 0 percent interest typically lasts only twelve to eighteen months, this strategy is best for short-term projects. The biggest risk and challenge of a 0 percent credit card is completing the project on time. If your project isn't completed on time, you'll end up paying a high interest rate on the money you charged. Be careful with your timing; it is okay to pay interest for a short period, but you want to avoid getting stuck with high interest rates for a long time. I would only recommend the credit card strategy if you have reserves you can use to pay those cards down, so you don't get stuck with higher interest.

If you pay balances down and threaten to cancel your card, several banks will reinstate the 0 percent promotion for another year or more. It's always worth trying. Make sure not to actually cancel the card, as that could negatively impact your credit score. I have had one card at 0 percent for over four years and counting!

Another negative about 0 percent personal cards is that if you use much more than 30 to 40 percent of the total available credit line, your credit score could drop. You may not need your credit for anything, and perhaps you're okay taking a temporary hit, as it does recover very quickly once you get it paid down. Only you can decide if it is worth the toll to save some interest.

BUSINESS CREDIT LINES AND CREDIT CARDS

Business credit cards can give you a lot of the same perks that personal cards can, but without a lot of the negatives. On the downside, you do need to have a business entity established to get business credit cards. Also, the 0 percent interest rate seems to not last as long for business credit cards, and they don't seem willing to give you extensions of the 0 percent rate as often as personal cards do. The biggest perk of the business card is that you can max them out, and it will not have any impact on your credit score! Business credit cards are perhaps the best tool for short-term fix-and-flip projects. Just as with personal credit cards, be careful to track the expiration date of your 0 percent interest card. You don't want to get stuck paying high interest.

Even better than credit cards, you can build a relationship with a bank and apply for a business line of credit. It works just like a credit card, but it's already as good as cash. Although you cannot get 0 percent on this type of business line, it also doesn't balloon up to 20 percent or more interest after nine to twelve months. Rather, it stays consistently at 8 to 12 percent. Like its credit card cousin, it doesn't impact your credit to max it out. I would suggest this is the best option of the unsecured credit lines.

KEY TAKEAWAYS

There are many sources of money you can tap into or help

others tap into to fund all the real estate deals you could find and manage. These sources include home equity credit lines, cash value life insurance, retirement accounts, 0 percent personal and business credit cards, and unsecured business credit lines.

In the next chapter, we'll look at using other people's money for deals, with a focus on hard money lenders and private money lenders.

TAKE ACTION EXERCISE:
TAKE STOCK OF POSSIBLE MONEY SOURCES

*(Download a printable version at
www.lambertbonus.com.)*

1. If you own a home, what do you think it's worth right now? What do you owe on the home?

2. Do you own any cash value life insurance (for example, whole life or indexed universal life)? If so, call your agent and find out how much is currently available and record that amount below.

3. Do you have an IRA, 401(k), or other retirement account set up through your employment? If so, call the account manager or human resource director and find out how much could be available to borrow and record it below. Likewise, if you have a personal retirement account or a retirement account with a previous employer, look it up and record the amount below.

4. What is your credit score? If it's 700-plus you could be a great fit to get some 0 percent personal and business credit cards or unsecured business credit lines. Schedule a call with me through www.lambertbonus. com, and I can show you how to maximize what you can get from these lines.

5. Adding up all the above amounts, as well as any savings you can use, what's the total amount that you have available for investment?

CHAPTER 7

BUYING PROPERTIES WITH OTHER PEOPLE'S MONEY

Chad had $200,000 in his savings account, and he wanted to use that money to flip houses. He was obsessed with the notion of not paying money lenders. After all, he had the money and could do this even if it meant tying up all his reserves. He found a deal and used his savings to flip the house, which took six months to complete. He made $30,000 on the flip. He couldn't start looking for another deal until the first deal was closed and paid out, because he couldn't risk not having funds available. The full process required between eight and ten months, meaning Chad was limited to an average of a little more than one deal a year. It was awful when Chad got a deal that lost money, because then all his surplus income was gone, and he felt very reluctant to keep putting his money at risk. Since all his savings were tied up in the deal, he recognized he could be putting his family in jeopardy with no reserves, causing a lot of stress.

* * *

Kapil had $200,000 in his savings account, but the last thing he wanted to do was to use that money. Kapil had an abundance mindset and was okay sharing a small part of the profit with a money lender. There was plenty of profit to go around, and he knew that by utilizing the lender's money he would be able to do far more deals than he could have otherwise. Instead of not being able to look for new deals until his funds were ready and available, Kapil was constantly looking for deals. He had an unlimited supply of money with enough hustle on his part. As a result, Kapil was always flipping between five and fourteen houses at a time. Yes, he sacrificed 10 to 20 percent of his profits to his lenders, but he more than made up for that through increased volume. Also, he felt secure knowing he had $200,000 stored away in a secure account he could draw upon if he ever had a loss. He was not as afraid of losses as Chad was, because he had the reserves ready to go if needed.

Who would you prefer to model your business after, Chad or Kapil? If you want to scale your business to a high level, you must use other people's money. In this chapter, I'll illustrate the importance of using other people's money on deals and show you several ways to raise money.

WHY YOU SHOULD NEVER USE YOUR OWN MONEY ON FLIPS

There are three major reasons why you should never use your own money on flips. First, using your own money limits how many deals you can actually do. Second, it turns your brain off of finding mode. Third, it limits the amount of money you have in reserve.

#1: LIMITS HOW MANY DEALS YOU CAN DO

If you're trying to do deals using your own money, you'll be extremely limited in what you are able to do. For instance, Chad, in the previous example, was only able to do a deal every eight months at the earliest. He had to wait for the project to complete before he could do another one. In contrast, when you use other people's money, you can have multiple projects going at once.

#2: TURNS YOUR BRAIN OFF OF FINDING MODE

A second problem with using your own money is that you're going to miss out on several potential deals. This is because you have turned off the finding antennae in your brain to look only when your funds are available. There could be a great number of deals that have passed you by that you simply didn't notice. You weren't seeing them, even when they were right in front of you. If you have the mentality of "I have unlimited money!" then deals are going to find you as soon as you're mentally ready to take them on.

#3: LIMITS YOUR RESERVES

One of the biggest mistakes many investors make is not having reserves. It's sometimes easy to see only the potential profits, but as you scale your business (which will be discussed in chapter 15), you're almost surely going to lose money on some deals. That is normal and natural, and you should not beat yourself up too hard. But it's important that you have reserves stashed away in a safe place, growing interest, so that you can handle these losses.

If you don't have reserves, you can get into a bad situation quickly. I have seen it happen with someone I know. He got into a bit of a mess and lost some money and didn't have the reserves to cover the loss. He decided to borrow money from someone else to pay for the loss. This is like robbing Peter to pay Paul! Then he had to borrow from someone else to pay the other guy. Well, it got to the point where it became a Ponzi scheme, and before you knew it, the Securities and Exchange Commission was onto him. He's now facing jail time. I think it began innocently. He was trying to dig himself out of a bad situation, and the bad turned ugly.

Never use other people's money for anything outside of what you said it would be used for. You will end up regretting it. You need and should have reserves on hand at all times. Please don't ever get into a position where you're using one person's money to fix a mistake on a different deal. Rather, use your own money for reserves to fix the problems, and then you'll stay safe.

OTHER PEOPLE'S MONEY IS MORE SACRED THAN YOUR OWN

Here's a word of caution to keep you out of trouble—other people's money should be treated more sacredly than your own money. It may be tempting when you are using other people's money to do deals or be sloppy on your research. After all, it's not your own money that's at stake. Instead, you should look at it like you've been given a sacred trust and you're the steward of these funds. Be doubly cautious to make sure the deal is good. I prefer to lose my own money rather than someone else's because it is the right thing to do. Your reputation is everything. Let me give you an example.

I was going on a trip and was skimpy on my research. I trusted several sources telling me the house could sell for XYZ, when in reality it wasn't worth as much. To make matters worse, the city shut down the project due to permitting issues. My partner, whose job it was to run the project, went missing in action for several months and didn't get the permit issue taken care of. Meanwhile, our hard money costs were eating us up. It turned out to be one of the rare times when I knew I was going to lose money—to the tune of $40,000. Ouch!

I had borrowed from a hard money lender (a role I will explain soon) and a private money individual to do the rehab. I was within my rights to tell the lenders, "So sorry, but I'm going to let you foreclose and take the property." I knew the hard money lender would not trust me in the future if I did that. Yet he could probably sell the property after foreclosing and recoup his money. However, the private money person in second position was going to lose most of his money if I didn't take responsibility for my deal going south. He trusted me, and there was no way I was going to let that trust be misplaced.

I did the right thing by selling the property at a lower price (your property will always sell at the right price). We had to bring $40,000 to the closing table to get it done. This was very painful, but I had the reserves to make it happen. Not only did I give both of my lenders their money back, but I also paid them all the interest I promised them. Both of them made some good money on the deal, while I took the total loss on my shoulders. Again, not only was doing this the right thing to do morally, but acting any other way would have hurt my reputation. Future lenders and other individuals wouldn't want to do a deal with me as a result.

This is the trade-off—using other people's money lets you achieve your financial independence goal more quickly, but you are responsible for that money. With this in mind, let's take a look at the two main types of lenders: hard money lender and private money lender.

HARD MONEY LENDER

A hard money lender is a professional investor who specializes in lending to other investors. The great thing about a hard money lender is that you don't have to have good credit or fill out a million forms to qualify. They base the qualifications on the property, not you, because they will get the property if you don't perform.

Most hard money lenders won't buy 100 percent of the property for you. You're going to need to come in with a 10 to 30 percent down payment. That's why you will usually also need private money, which I'll talk about next. Hard money lenders do this to protect themselves, in case you mess up. They can foreclose and sell the property to get their money back. They usually charge 2 to 3 percent of the loan amount as "origination points" (a finance charge by the lender) and then a 10 to 16 percent annualized interest rate. Most will charge an extra origination point or two after a certain period, like six months.

It is not cheap money. However, if you don't have enough profit margin in the deal to pay a hard money lender, you shouldn't be doing the deal in the first place.

PRIVATE MONEY LENDER

Private money lenders are typically not professional investors. They are ordinary people who are looking to get a good return on their money, backed by real estate. For instance, your Uncle Kent or nurse, Jen, could be your private money investor. The rate on private money is completely negotiable but usually falls within the range of 6 to 12 percent without origination points.

If the private money individual is willing to lend you large amounts of money, then you will not need a hard money lender at all. Usually, though, private money is used to supplement a hard money lender. Many call the private money loan "gap funding" because it fills the gap between what the hard money lender is willing to put down and the purchase price.

Private money is usually in second position, unless there is no hard money lender involved. This means that if the investor messes up, the person in first position gets first claim to get paid back upon the sale of the property. If there's money left over, the person or entity in second position gets paid. If you become a private money investor, it's important to work with a seasoned investor who will be better at selecting profitable deals and will have reserves. Don't give your money to people who don't have reserves.

EXAMPLE OF HARD AND PRIVATE MONEY IN ACTION

Let's imagine that you find a very good deal. You get a contract with a seller to buy his property for $200,000. You then send that contract to a hard money lender with your estimate of how much you think it will cost to fix it up. You also let her know what you think it will sell for, upon completion, based on recent comparable sales in that neighborhood. The hard money lender will verify the information, and if she likes it, she will then give you a percentage of the purchase price. In this scenario, she may give you $170,000 with two origination points and 12 percent annual interest. All this can happen within days! You will then need to come up with the extra $30,000 to buy it and whatever additional funds you need to fix it up. Let's say you need $25,000 to fix up the property in this scenario.

Next, you contact your private money investor and let him know you need $55,000 for a deal. You show them the numbers of your projected profits and what interest rate you will give. Let's say you decide on 10 percent. You sign paperwork to put a lien on the property in the private money person's name or entity. This ensures that you can't sell the property without paying him back with the promised interest.

When the day comes to close on the property, both the hard money lender and private money lender wire funds to your title company. You sign all the paperwork, and then the title company wires you the remaining $25,000 that you will use to pay all your contractors.

You complete the renovations, and six months later you sell the property for $300,000. Upon closing, you need to pay the hard and private money lenders their share. Your paperwork with the hard money lender states two origination points (2 percent) of $170,000 and 12 percent annualized interest for six months. Thus, you owe the hard money lender $3,400 for the origination points and $10,200 for the interest, for a total of $13,600. The hard money lender throws in some extra fees as well to make a little more money. Your private money lender rate was 10 percent of $55,000. Annualized, that is $5,500 for the full year or $2,750 for six months. Thus, your total money costs on this deal would be $16,350. If you had completed it in four months, it would be even less. As you can see, time really is money, and you need to make sure your crew is getting the work done as quickly as possible. Finally, let's say you paid realtors $12,000 to sell it and incurred $5,000 in closing costs.

The good news is since you sold this property for $300,000, you're still making around $42,000 profit even after paying your lenders a premium fee. The return for you is technically infinite because you invested none of your own money into the deal!

HOW TO RAISE MONEY FOR DEALS

Raising money for deals is not as hard as it sounds, and you'd be surprised how many people will be excited to invest in real estate with you. Following are a few ideas.

GOLD IN YOUR BACKYARD

You'd be shocked at how many people you already know who would be willing to be your money partner on a deal. You simply need to have the courage to ask them. I'd start by broadcasting your real estate passion on social media. Let people know you're serious and want to get deals. Next, make a spreadsheet list of everyone you know and ask them all if they'd be interested in investing in real estate with you. If they show an interest, let them know you're looking at several deals. Request their permission to contact them with the numbers when you find something promising.

When you do find a good deal, send them a prospectus on your projections about the deal and what you would be willing to give them for their participation. If it is a long-term rental, most people are going to want an equity position. You could make them your 50/50 partner, sharing all the benefits of the deal. If it is a short-term fix and flip, you may be better off to give them a guaranteed annualized return that you two negotiate together. I recommend beginning by asking them what they would like. If a 6 percent return sounds good to them, it definitely works for you!

Make sure you secure their money by putting a lien on the property when you buy it. Your title company can draft that for you. A lien legally ties up the property so that the seller is required to get the lien released before the property can be sold.

NETWORKING EVENTS

Another great resource for raising capital is to attend networking events. It is best if it's a real estate investing-focused networking event. If you live in Atlanta, Georgia, you could type into your internet search engine: "Real estate investing association, Atlanta." You'll likely see different websites of meetups where you can connect with other investors and find hard money and private money lenders. You will also find partners for deals and people to be on your investing team to help transact your deals.

I am a part of a huge, nationwide real estate investing community. If you want to schedule a free call with me or one of my team members to learn more about it, go to www. lambertbonus.com. The contacts in my group could also be potential money partners for deals. I have raised several million dollars from this group while making lasting friendships and helping many to get started on their journey.

KEY TAKEAWAYS

By using other people's money for deals, you can work on several deals simultaneously and keep your mind in finding mode. Plus, it lets you keep your own money in reserve to cover potential losses. You should treat other people's money as more sacred than your own, so reserves are critical.

The two main sources of lending are hard money lenders and private money lenders. For most deals, you will use a combination of both. The best ways to raise funds are by talking to people you already know or by making new contacts at networking events. Connecting with willing money lenders will give you confidence to find more deals and get you to financial independence so much faster.

Using other people's money isn't the only way to buy properties. You can also use other people's mortgages by buying *Subject To*, as we'll explore in the next chapter.

TAKE ACTION EXERCISE:
USING OTHER PEOPLE'S MONEY

*(Download a printable version at
www.lambertbonus.com.)*

1. Write about one or two things you found most helpful in this chapter that you want to apply to your career.

2. What would be your preferred method of raising money?

3. List five people you think may be open to being a lender for you.

CHAPTER 8

BUYING HOMES WITH OTHER PEOPLE'S MORTGAGES

Amy was behind six months on her mortgage and was about to lose her house and everything she cared about to the bank and become homeless. Her daughter's medical bills had caused her not to be able to make payments. To make matters worse, she had a mental disorder that led to hoarding. There was literally junk piled up three to four feet high throughout the house. You couldn't even make it into the kitchen or most of the bedrooms. There was no chance any regular buyer would even consider this property, so Amy was really stuck in a hard position and was about to lose her credit and everything she owned to the bank.

Keith, one of my elite investor team members, knocked on Amy's door and set up an appointment for us to meet with her. We presented Amy with a solution. We would send the money to the bank to catch her up on her mortgage. We would give her several thousand dollars to get back on her feet and to find a place to rent. We would not only save her credit from the seven-year stain of foreclosure but would give her lifesaving funds to start again. Furthermore, we'd take her home in its current condition. She wouldn't have to do anything aside from packing up what she wanted to take with her. In exchange, she would deed the property to us *Subject To* her existing mortgage. Amy would stay on the mortgage, but we would be named on the title. We'd make the payments directly to her bank on her behalf, which would really help her credit recover. This was a lot cheaper for us than having to get a hard money loan to buy the property.

It was quite a project. We removed fourteen dumpsters' worth of piled up junk from the house. The stench could be smelled a block away as my crew pulled out three dead cats and all kinds of rotten stuff. Some of the floors had rotted, and it was quite a project to fix it up. Yet, in the end, my partner and I split about $50,000! It was a win for everyone involved!

WHAT IS *SUBJECT TO*?

Subject To means that the seller stays on the mortgage but transfers the title to you as the buyer. In other words, you buy the property *Subject To* the existing mortgage, and you make payments to the bank on behalf of the seller. You get all the tax benefits and have full control of the property, even though the debt isn't in your name.

BENEFITS OF *SUBJECT TO* FOR THE BUYER

There are many benefits of buying a property *Subject To* for the buyer:

1. You can buy an unlimited number of properties with financing already in place.
2. You get the tax benefits.
3. You don't have to use expensive hard money because cheaper bank financing is already in place.
4. You can rent the property, flip the property, or even sell it on terms to someone else and still make a profit in the middle.

BENEFITS OF *SUBJECT TO* FOR THE SELLER

There are also multiple benefits for the seller:

1. Their credit can be saved from foreclosure.
2. Their credit can improve as you make payments on their behalf.
3. If you ever stop making payments, they can get their house back with all its equity.

4. They can get money quickly, as these kinds of sales go through very fast.
5. They can sell you the house in any condition and don't have to do expensive and time-consuming renovations before selling it to you.

HOW TO CONVINCE THE SELLER ON *SUBJECT TO*

A lot of sellers will be very skeptical of selling a property to you on *Subject To*. My favorite group of people to help are those who have a notice of default on their property. These individuals are in a bad position and are about to lose their house and all their equity. To get these individuals on board, here are a few things you can do:

1. Build rapport and trust by asking about their situation and listening with empathy.
2. Let them know you can catch them up with the bank to save their credit from foreclosure and give them some money to get them back on their feet.
3. Emphasize they don't even need to clean their house and you will get them cash fast.
4. Point out that you will help their credit as you make payments on their behalf.
5. Let them know that if you ever miss payments, they can get their house back, all caught up with the bank and with all the improvements you make.

6. Show them you're using a state-approved contract and these transactions are done by realtors all the time.

I have acquired several dozen properties through the *Subject To* method and, although there is a learning curve to this method, it's worth it.

KEY TAKEAWAYS

Going with traditional bank methods, you can only get ten properties in your name, according to Fannie Mae and Freddie Mac mortgage guidelines. Getting to ten is very difficult. The banks want you to show a high amount of reserves with every new property, and they have mountains of paperwork. Yet buying a home *Subject To* someone else's existing mortgage is a phenomenal way to fully control a property without ever having to deal with a bank. It can be a means of acquiring an unlimited number of properties! There are so many benefits of this method to both the seller and to the buyer. Learning how to have an effective conversation about it will set you on the path to financial independence.

In the next chapter, we'll look at another alternative to finding money: partnering with other people and using their credit.

TAKE ACTION EXERCISE:
THE *SUBJECT TO* STRATEGY

*(Download a printable version at
www.lambertbonus.com.)*

1. Write about one or two things you found most helpful
   in this chapter that you want to apply to your career.

2. What do you find most appealing about the *Subject
   To* strategy?

3. Practice your conversation; list all the ways a seller-
   financed property could benefit the seller.

CHAPTER 9

BUYING HOMES WITH OTHER PEOPLE'S CREDIT

I had purchased my first rental property on my own credit, and I had a little money left in my home equity line of credit. On my professor's salary, I wasn't going to be able to qualify for another loan, nor did I have enough money for a large down payment. Yet I wanted to get my next deal and I was anxious to make it happen. I had shared my investing story with another professor, named Bryce. He was interested in doing something similar but was a little unsure where to look and how to make it happen. I suggested we do one together. I would pitch in a little money and help find the deal, and we'd use his credit and split the equity. It worked out fantastically well, and we still own this property eight years later. I now have more than a dozen credit partners and have had few problems.

Unless you have a war chest filled with millions of dollars, there's no way you're going to buy dozens of properties without working with others in some capacity. Credit partnership can be a powerful win for both partners and get both of you further in the game than either of you could have done on your own.

Leveraging other people's credit can help you reach your financial independence number of properties quickly. In this chapter, I'll show you how you can partner with friends or acquaintances to get more rental properties.

PARTNERSHIP POWER: DIVIDE THE WORK

There are many elements of a deal, but fortunately, you don't have to do them all on your own. With a credit partner, the two of you can divide the work.

You are typically much better off specializing and getting good at one or two of the elements of a deal, and working with a credit partner who brings other skills to the table. Here are the six key elements of a deal:

1. **Finding**. Good deals are not easy to come by. Proficiency at finding below-market deals is a huge contribution someone can make to a partnership.
2. **Credit**. I always recommend using cheaper bank financing for long-term deals. Your return on invest-

ment goes way down when you use cash to buy a deal. Not to mention most people don't have millions of dollars in cash to finance deals long term. If you don't have cheaper bank financing available to you, as was the case for me in the opening story, a credit partner is great and expands your options of what you can buy.

3. **Money.** I have purchased one property with no money out of pocket, but it's very rare. Usually, you're going to need some sort of down payment. When purchasing with bank financing, you're more than likely to need 20 percent down. Remember, it doesn't have to be your money! Again, a partner can come in handy here.

4. **Management.** Likely, the house you buy will need some level of rehab done before it is ready to rent. This requires managing contractors and seeing a deal through. This might be a skill you bring to the table, or it might be something you'd rather have a partner take care of.

5. **Rent/sale.** Once the property has been rehabbed, it will need to be marketed for either rental or for sale. There's a lot of work involved in talking to potential renter/buyers and lots of paperwork to be completed. Again, if this is something you're good at, great! If not, a partner can help.

6. **Expertise.** Having an experienced partner is a huge asset. The experienced partner can make sure the deal is on track for a good profit. Experience gives assurance you are taking everything needed into account.

You don't know what you don't know. Having someone help out to both avoid rough situations and deal with them when they arise is priceless. Someone with expertise can bring a wealth of contacts, systems, and vision to make a deal successful.

Again, the great thing about real estate is that you can be part of a deal if all you bring to the table is even one of these six major roles. All the better if you can master two or more. If you get good at one or more of them, you can make a career of it and bring in a lot of wealth for your family. But you'll need to find partners who complement your strengths and help you with the remaining elements of the deal.

BENEFITS THAT CAN BE SHARED WITH A PARTNER

Just as there are many roles to a deal that you can divide with a partner, there are also many benefits to real estate that can be divided in any way the two of you want. Here are the key benefits you can divide how you want:

1. **Cash flow**. After all the expenses are considered, the net profit from the rent represents monthly cash flow.
2. **Appreciation**. Over time, the value of the property will most likely increase.
3. **Tax benefits**. You can depreciate the property on your taxes (see chapter 17) over 27.5 years. If you're a real estate professional (you spend 750 hours a year, four-

teen hours a week on real estate endeavors), you can get a huge tax write-off through accelerated depreciation of close to 25 percent of the purchase price. You also get a deduction for mortgage interest.

4. **Equity**. As the mortgage is paid down by the tenants, the equity in the property increases.

5. **Use**. If the property is a short-term vacation rental, one or both partners may want to visit the property for free.

Again, these are the core benefits of the property that can be divided however you want in whatever percentage you agree to.

HOW TO HAVE A DISCUSSION WITH A CREDIT PARTNER

Before entering a deal with a credit partner, it's important to have a discussion to make sure you're on the same page. I recommend the following steps:

1. Find a deal that will provide cash flow.
2. Create a document that illustrates to your credit partner all the expenses and all the potential profit of the deal.
3. Discuss some of the benefits (as described in the previous section) and some of the risks with the potential partner. A risk is losing money if you don't have reserves in place and have to sell during a down market. A

common concern is that tenants may trash the place, but this is easily remedied with insurance.

4. Find out what the most important benefit to the credit partner is. It could be cash flow, equity, or tax benefits. If possible, give them as much as you can of what they want the most, especially if it is not the same as what you want most.

5. Have a lender ready and get the credit partner preapproved with this lender right away if they agree to do the deal with you.

Many deals await you as you partner with like-minded individuals to crush it together.

KEY TAKEAWAYS

Credit partners can be an incredible resource for expanding your portfolio much more quickly. They can also contribute far more than credit alone. There are so many ways to contribute to a deal and so many elements of a deal can be divided up. Start having conversations with potential credit partners right away and get some deals rolling.

In the next chapter, we'll cover one of my favorite strategies for finding money for deals—house hacking!

TAKE ACTION EXERCISE:
CREDIT PARTNERSHIPS

*(Download a printable version at
www.lambertbonus.com.)*

1. Write about one or two things you found most helpful in this chapter that you want to apply to your career.

2. List five people who could be credit partners for you.

3. What main parts of the deal are most important to you between tax write-offs, appreciation, cash flow, or equity?

CHAPTER 10

HOUSE HACKING INTO A DEAL

Robert, a member of my elite investing team, was moving to a new state and had a very large family with thirteen children. He wanted to get a large home, but he also wanted to have a payment that would be affordable. Robert was able to get a 5,500-square-foot home under contract and even found a family friend to finance it for him. The home had a very large basement, which he converted to a rental property. Robert was able to live upstairs in a much bigger space than before for approximately the same payment as before. This was due to his house hack!

As another example, while looking to buy my dream house, I wanted to do it in a smart way. I examined the short-term Airbnb rental potential of my current home and found out it was going to be a home run! It would produce around $5,100 a month. After my mortgage payment of $2,000, I would get about $3,100 in cash flow. Next, I found my dream house—nine thousand square feet in the foothills of the mountains with a large theater room, three kitchens, three laundry rooms, a sports court, and a guest house. It was everything my wife and I had ever dreamed of! Even better, the guest house included an accessory apartment with rental potential of around $1,150. My new mortgage payment on the dream house would be $4,780. The $3,100 in cash flow from my old house combined with $1,150 from renting out the guest house would be $4,250 in cash flow. This would make my new net payment only $530. In other words, the size of my home would increase by 300 percent, but my monthly payment would decrease by almost 400 percent. Now that's a house hack!

HOUSE HACK ANALYSIS

SHORT TERM AIRBNB
Mortgage - $2,000
Income - $3,100

DREAM HOUSE
Mortgage - $4,780
Income - $1,150

Total Income = $4,250
REMAINING HOUSE PAYMENT = $530

*Home increased in size **almost 300%** and the monthly payment **decreased 400%**!*

Unfortunately, a situation with a neighbor nixed our plan to rent our old house. Instead, we sold it for $103,000 profit, but that's what projections were. We did rent out the guest house for $1,150, so we still are doing a house hack. House hacking is the easiest way to get into your first property. Let's discuss the details of how to pull this off!

WHAT IS A HOUSE HACK?

My definition of a house hack is finding a way to rent out part of your current house. You could make an official separate-entrance rental, or even rent out a room in your house. A double house hack is when you can turn your current house into a rental, move into a new house, *and* rent out part of that new house. This could do wonders for your monthly cash flow! Someone else will be making all or part of your mortgage payments for you!

I have not met someone who has done this yet, but you could create as many as five new rental spaces through house hacking. For example, let's say you made a separate entrance in your current home and rented out two units. Then, you might move into a fourplex, where you could live in one unit while renting out the other three. You could even get cheap noncommercial financing on such a deal! Please, if anyone reading this book can execute the 5× house hack, please message me about it!

CREATING A HOUSE HACK

First, talk to your spouse or anyone else you live with about the possibility of renting out a room or creating a separate entrance for part of your house. The benefit could be large if you're willing to sacrifice a little bit of privacy.

Then check your city ordinances. Some cities are pretty laid back about this kind of thing, but others are uptight. You do not want to put too much money into a house hack if the city is going to crack down on you. One easy way to tell is to search your area as a potential Airbnb guest. If there are few or no Airbnb's available, chances are ordinances may be strict. You can also call the planning and zoning office to ask about any ordinances prohibiting renting out a portion of your house. However, even when cities do have such ordinances, they often don't enforce them, so you should also talk to other investors in your area for guidance.

When looking for a house hack to move into, the easiest thing to do is to search the internet for "the city you want to move to" and "mother-in-law apartments." For example, "Salt Lake City, mother-in-law apartments." In my area, someone had already put a website together that had all the current listings with mother-in-law apartments! You could also contact a realtor and have them make a hot sheet that would send you listings that have mother-in-law apartments. These are great because you don't have to go through the hassle and expense of adding a kitchen. It is already built in. If your spouse is willing to live in a triplex or a fourplex, you can have a realtor send those listings as well. The realtor can also help you negotiate a good deal.

HOW TO STRUCTURE A HOUSE HACK

To structure a successful house hack, I recommend you first do a rental analysis on your current or future property. Get some projections about what it could look like. I describe in great depth how to do this analysis in chapter 12.

You can look at it as a short-term vacation rental or a long-term rental. AirDNA could help you make a projection about the short-term rental. A website such as Rentometer could give you insight about what the long-term rental picture would be like. Subtract your projected monthly mortgage payment from the projected rental payment. This will give you your gross cash flow. If you want a management company, factor that in, as well as vacancy and repairs. I have met many people who ended up living payment-free, as the rent covered their mortgage payment for their new place. This was how I survived on my measly professor salary.

An important factor to consider when deciding on a house hack is the parking situation. You will most likely get into trouble with the city if a neighbor complains. The biggest issue that would trigger a complaint would be on-street parking. If you don't have enough potential parking, you're going to want to add some, if possible, or consider a different property if it doesn't make sense to add any.

KEY TAKEAWAYS

House hacking is the easiest way to get into your first deal. All it requires is that you have a room or separate entrance and are willing to sacrifice the space to make some cash. To take it to the next level, find a new house that has a mother-in-law apartment that you could turn into a rental. Then rent out your old space and you have created two rentals with one move. The following Take Action Exercise will help you determine whether a potential house hack makes sense for you.

Now that we've looked at all the different ways to find the money needed to make deals, in the next part of the book, we'll dive into the nuts and bolts of executing deals, starting with how to find them in the first place.

TAKE ACTION EXERCISE:
HOUSE HACKING

(Download a printable version at
www.lambertbonus.com.)

1. Write about one or two things you found most helpful in this chapter that you want to apply to your career.

2. Have you considered moving?

3. Would you be open to renting out part of your house?

4. If you rented out a room in your house or sectioned off an apartment in your current house, what does AirDNA or Rentometer suggest it could rent for?

5. What would your new net payment on your house be if you were able to rent a portion of it?

PART III

NUTS AND BOLTS OF THE DEAL

CHAPTER 11

FIVE CORE WAYS OF FINDING THE DEAL

Edmund was frustrated and messaged me, letting me know he was not finding the kind of deals he would like to be finding. I asked him where he was looking, and he said he was looking at the multiple listing service (MLS), where all properties are bought and sold. I told him he was looking in the wrong place and that it is nearly impossible to find a deal on the MLS. He needed to look at sources off the MLS. I reminded him of some of the amazing software I provide to help investors find those who are very motivated to sell at a discount. I also told him he should be bold and let people on social media know he was doing real estate and open up about it. He took my advice and, within a week, one of his family members had approached him about being in trouble with their mortgage. He did that deal, and he and his partner made $26,000, the first of a dozen or so in his first year working with me!

Finding a deal—a property at a steep enough discount that you can make a good profit—is one of the first and important steps in your investing journey. It can also be the most difficult step, and it is the place where many people give up. There are many dozens of ways to find deals, but in this chapter, I will describe five of the most successful methods and point out their pros and cons. Make sure to read to the end of the chapter, because number five works the best for me and for members of my elite investing team.

As you read through these strategies, I want you to analyze which of these methods seems to be the best fit for your personality. Then, spend at least five hours each week engaging in that strategy as your finding focus. At first, you won't know what to say to potential sellers, but you will get better with practice. Also, if you reach out to me, I can connect you with some great scripts (www.lambertbonus.com).

#1: KNOCKING ON DOORS

There is software that compiles county records where you can see who has a notice of default on their property. They are behind on their mortgage; they're about to lose all their equity, and get smacked with the black mark of a foreclosure on their record. The software compiles other lead types as well, but my favorite focus is on the notice of default or a pre-foreclosure. The software provides you with the name and address of everyone in your area who is in trouble. (For up-to-date software recommendations, visit www.lambertbonus.com.)

You can create a driving route to swing by each of these properties and knock on their door. Start a conversation based on what you'll learn in the next chapter. If nobody answers, leave a handwritten note to let them know you'd like to help them out of their situation. Include your contact info.

If possible, get creative and leave them something memorable, because there will likely be others who are also trying to contact them. For instance, you might leave a fake $100 bill with a miniature Nestle Crunch bar with a note that says, "I know you're in a cash crunch, and I'd like to help you out." At one house, Mason, one of my elite investing team members, left a flower and a note saying, "I'd like to help you turn another leaf." We made about $50,000 when we sold that house! These are a few ideas to increase the chance you will get a callback.

Pros. It's hard to replace the rapport you can build by talking to someone face-to-face. You can break the ice by talking about what they like and don't like in the neighborhood. You may be able to get into the house, look around, and get a contract signed right then. Having seen the house, you'll have an idea of what you could pay for it, and you're going to be ahead of the competition who hasn't built face-to-face rapport. Some studies say up to 55 percent of communication is through body language,[1] so you will get the full communication when you knock on the door.

Cons. It can be terrifying to knock on a door and wonder if someone will slam the door in your face (and occasionally they will be rude). I am an extreme extrovert and even I was pretty terrified at first, so this method isn't for the faint of heart. It can involve a lot of driving around, and sometimes, someone might not even open the door. This can feel less efficient than other methods.

DIALING

The phone can be a little more comfortable for many people looking to make contact with potential leads. You can still build a fair amount of rapport over the phone, since vocal intonations account for around 38 percent of communication.[2] You could use the software to find the names of individuals in pre-foreclosure. Then you could use a website like familytreenow.com to find their phone numbers.

---

1   Jeff Thompson, "Is Nonverbal Communication a Numbers Game?" *Psychology Today*, September 30, 2011, https://www.psychologytoday.com/us/blog/beyond-words/201109/is-nonverbal-communication-numbers-game.

2   Ibid.

You could also reach lead sources, such as out-of-state land-lords, by phone, which you can't do by knocking.

Another way of reaching people by phone is to make calls from your local classifieds, like Craigslist. One type of potential lead you can find from the classifieds are *for sale by owner* properties—those trying to avoid selling through a realtor. A lot of these people want a pie-in-the-sky price for their home. You don't want to buy this type of property unless you can get an amazing discount. Some won't have even talked to a realtor or may not know the market value on their home. A few of them could be very motivated to sell right away, due to the poor condition of their home or other external factors.

My cousin Conner joined my elite investing team and called a classified ad. He then brought me in to help negotiate the deal. We were able to talk this client into selling a triplex to us for only $10,000 down on seller finance. We cash flowed $300 a month for two years. We then decided to sell the property and made $62,000. All this started with a simple phone call.

You could also call people who are listing their property for rent and ask them if they would be open to a rent-to-own. Let them know you could make a significant down payment rather than a deposit. Tell them they would not have to worry about maintenance and repairs. This is a great way to buy the property *Subject To* or on seller financing! (The main difference between *Subject To* and seller finance is a *Subject To* seller has a bank loan, while a seller-finance seller owns the property outright.)

Pros. You can still build some rapport with tonality on the phone, and you can reach more people without having to drive to each potential seller. There's still some pain from rejection, but it's easier to have someone hang up on you than to have the door slammed in your face.

Cons. You may have to go through a lot of bad phone numbers to actually reach someone. You're still missing out on 55 percent of communication by not having the body language. If you can get good enough at building rapport over the phone, you can make up for the lack of in-person communication.

MAILING

If you have some funds to spare and don't have either the time or the desire to make cold contacts, you could pay to make your phone ring. Some of the software programs that collect leads also have done-for-you mailing campaigns. All you have to do is select the lead source you want to use, input your contact information, hit send, and you're done. Everything else happens automatically.

Don't send one mailer and expect you're going to get a lot of response. Studies show that often you need to send six to ten pieces of mail before someone will reply. Remember, words make up only about 7 percent of communication[3] and they're getting letters from many other people. You've got to stand out by being the person who consistently sends them something. When they call, you better answer or call them back as soon as possible. Then get good at building rapport over the phone and at setting up an in-person meeting.

Pros. Mailers don't take much of your time, and you don't have to deal with as much rejection. If you're willing to spend a lot of money, you could generate a lot of phone calls and good leads. If you want to scale your business, this is how a lot of the big-time investors grease the skids. This is the most efficient way to find deals.

Cons. It can be expensive, and usually you can only expect a 1 to 2 percent response rate, sometimes even lower. You cast a wide net with the worst form of communication and lose a lot of folks. There are a lot of people you're losing along the way in the process. The competition is steep. You'll be up against people who are spending $30,000 to $100,000-plus a month on mailers and have professionally trained closers.

---

3   Ibid.

WHOLESALERS

A wholesaler is a professional investor who often spends between $30,000 and $100,000-plus a month on mailers. Many get smoking-hot deals under contract. They then add an assignment fee of between $5,000 and $50,000 (sometimes more) and sell it to you after their markup.

You'll have a lot of competition with the big-time wholesalers. Most of these sellers have paid to get a massive mailing list of potential buyers (like you) to whom they send their deals and ask for the highest bidder. Oftentimes, there are people with huge amounts of cash on their wholesale lists that don't have to worry about money costs. They can pay more than you should pay for a property.

If you can find a newbie wholesaler who does not have a big list, you're likely to make a better margin on what they sell you. Also, these newbie wholesalers are going to be happy to make a couple thousand and might leave more meat on the bone for you. However, they're much less likely to find good deals.

You can connect with all types of wholesalers at networking meetings and investor club meetings. You can also search in Facebook groups or online.

Pros. Don't like knocking on doors, making calls, and spending gobs of money on marketing or time figuring out how to negotiate the deal yourself? Let the wholesalers do it. You will simply make a smaller margin of profit. Since many of these people are professionals, they may have gotten a much better discount than you could have anyway.

Cons. Wholesalers are assigning the contract to you and have a limited time window to sell the property. If you don't perform, they have to renegotiate an extended deadline with the seller. They've all been burned by would-be buyers that chickened out of a property, and then they ran out of time trying to sell it to another investor. Because of this, many wholesalers require a nonrefundable earnest money deposit, sometimes in high amounts such as $5,000. Given the limited time frames, about the only due diligence you can do is walk through it once and maybe sneak your inspector in for a quick look. So you often need to risk buying a house with unknown flaws and be willing to eat it. This is more of an "as is" sale.

Another con is that most wholesalers are going to present you with only the rosiest comparable properties. They will also give rosy projections about the amount of work that needs to be done. You can't trust anything they give you except the address, and you need to run your own analysis. Never trust the analysis of someone who stands to make a profit from selling you a property. Even if they are honest people, there's always bias that makes them want to tell the story that makes them the most money. The few deals I've lost money on have all come from wholesalers, so *be careful*. That is why, if you choose this finding method, you've got to get good at property analysis, which we'll talk about in the next chapter. Despite all these cons, I do get some of my deals from wholesalers, because I value my time and don't want to do all the marketing to find the deal myself.

Pro tip. If you've spent the time to analyze a wholesale deal, I recommend sending the wholesaler a text or email with the price you can pay. I've had wholesaler friends say that more people should make offers, because some of the wholesalers' deals don't fly off the shelves. They often come back to the lower offers, and if you didn't put one in, you'll never get those.

WARM CONTACTS

Okay, so I've saved the best for last. What I'm about to tell you has been my number one source of deals and it seems to be the number one source of the members of my elite investor team. Go to the people who know you and trust you, because they can be an amazing source, not only for deals but for raising money to do deals and for partnerships.

For instance, Eric, a member of my elite investor team, recently mentioned to one of his employees that he was now doing real estate. That individual urgently needed to move to Oregon. He was willing to sell his property (*Subject*

To) to Eric for what he owed the bank. In other words, Eric picked up this property with nothing out of pocket except closing costs! It all happened because he mentioned to someone he was becoming an investor. There are a few key steps to get leads flowing with this method.

DECLARE YOURSELF AN INVESTOR ON SOCIAL MEDIA

It's great to declare you're a real estate investor on social media. It can be a simple post, but let them know why you've chosen this path and how excited you would be to help people out of tough situations. Share some of the things you're learning in this book and talk about some of the deals you're looking at. The more you can get people to identify you as an investor, the more they're going to bring deals to you when something comes up.

MAKE A LIST

Make a list of everyone you have ever known or connected with during your life. I know it may sound daunting, but it's so important. You won't believe how many of them will be interested in real estate investing in some form or fashion. Google "memory jogger" and there are online tools to help you remember all your contacts. In a spreadsheet, write down their names, contact info, and how they best like to be contacted. Create a final column for notes for your follow-up.

Everyone you contact from your warm contacts list will fall into one of these four boxes or categories: Active Investor, Passive Money Partner / Credit Partner, Deal Provider, or Not Ready Yet. Make contact with each of these individuals by phone, text, online messenger—whatever feels most natural. Ask them the golden question: "Have you ever been interested in real estate investing?" If they say yes, you can ask the next question: "Are you more interested in actively finding deals *or* passively getting checks secured by real estate?" Their answer to that question will determine if they fit into one of the next two boxes.

Active Investor. If they say they are interested in actively finding deals, then they are going to be an Active Investor partner. You can share this book with them and connect them with knowledge and resources. They can be your accountability partner, your credit partner, money partner, or deal-finding partner. The synergy you can get working with these people you're connected with from your past will be so much fun.

Passive Money Partner/Credit Partner. If they're too busy to get involved, and they have some money, you could help them learn how to access their money to invest with you (see chapter 6). You've found a Passive Money Partner. Ask them if you can reach out to them when you have a deal ready to go. You're knocking out two birds with one stone.

Before you get off the phone with them, make sure to ask the following questions.

Deal Provider. To find out if they need help or can connect you to someone who needs your services, ask the first question: "Whom do you know who is struggling to make their mortgage payment or is planning to move in the next thirty to sixty days?" Give some examples! It could be their neighbor or someone at their work, their church, or their gym. If they give a name, get that person's contact info, and connect with the person. If they say nobody (and most will), ask them the second question: "Could you do me a favor and let me know if you ever come across someone who needs help?" If they agree, they will now be consciously or at least subconsciously searching for deals for you!

Not Ready Yet. The final box is for those who are neither interested in real estate yet nor do they know anyone who needs help from someone like us. Many of these individuals will come around later. For instance, Mason, one of the members of my elite investor team, turned me down several times. Yet he watched me on social media until finally he reached out to me and said he was ready to become an active real estate investor. We have done three deals together!

Pros. You're going to be able to use leverage to get more deals done by having other people find them for you. You'll

work with people you already know and rekindle old friendships. It's the easiest way to find deals, and you'll also find
money and investing partners all at once, killing three birds
with one stone! Also, it's free and requires much less in the
way of skills because your relationship smooths over some
of your lack of skill out of the gate.

Cons. The main con in this method is some people may
find it uncomfortable to approach people they know. You
may fear rejection from someone you care about more than
being rejected by a stranger. Don't let the initial discomfort
stop you. I usually remind myself that I was probably never
going to connect with this person again anyway. If so, what
does it matter if they turn me down?

KEY TAKEAWAYS

Finding properties at a steep discount is definitely not easy
but will come to those who take action consistently. The five
primary ways of finding deals include knocking on doors,
making calls, sending mailers, connecting with wholesalers,
or (the very best) connecting with your warm contacts and
asking them about their interest in real estate. Each method
has its pros and its cons, and you need to decide what you're
going to do and try it for at least six weeks in a row. If you
jump from one method to the next to the next, you'll never
gain any traction. There's a little bit of a learning curve to
each one. Carve out at least five hours in your schedule to

engage in one or two of these finding activities every week. Everything works if you work it.

After you find a deal, your next step is to analyze that deal and determine whether you can make a profit. In the next chapter, I'll give you a lightning deal analysis strategy to do just that.

TAKE ACTION EXERCISE: YOUR FINDING STRATEGY

(Download a printable version at www.lambertbonus.com.)

1. Write about one or two things you found most helpful in this chapter that you want to apply to your career.

2. What finding strategy appeals most to your personality and resources?

3. Can you commit to spending five hours a week finding and analyzing properties?

4. What is your ideal time of day when you will schedule these finding hours?

CHAPTER 12

LIGHTNING DEAL ANALYSIS

In addition to building my real estate portfolio, I spend a lot of my time helping new investors to learn the ropes. I was talking to Rafael and he loved the fact that I have weekly deal analysis sessions with my elite investor team. He was interested in my mentoring, but in the end, he was unwilling to invest in himself. I was pretty heartbroken when he messaged me a few weeks later and told me about a deal he had purchased. He had miscalculated his numbers and was about to lose $25,000 and wondered if there was any way out of it. Unfortunately, there was not, and I felt bad that he had to get educated by the school of hard knocks. I knew this was probably something he would not recover from. He probably wouldn't try investing again after this type of scarring loss.

After you find the deal, you must know how to determine whether it will get you a favorable return on investment. Getting the numbers right on a deal is crucial, and you don't know what you don't know. If you get your numbers wrong, it can be very costly indeed. It is worth really learning how to do this and practicing with a mentor until you make sure you're getting it right.

The aim of this chapter is to help you learn how to do some quick analyses on properties to determine what you can offer on the property. Once you do your due diligence, you can hammer out every cost and get more of an exact number on the total cost.

THREE STEPS TO ANALYZING A FLIP

The ability to do a lightning analysis of a property is important in the world of fix and flips. To successfully do this, you need to focus on three core steps.

#1: DETERMINE THE AFTER-REPAIR VALUE

The after-repair value is the first important step to figuring out what your offer can be. Here are a few guidelines to consider:

- Look at properties that are fixed up in the condition that you want to sell your flip.

- Ideally, find something within a one-half mile to mile radius of the subject property.
- If possible, find homes that are plus or minus 10 percent the size of the subject property.
- If possible, find something that has sold within three to six months.
- Focus primarily on the "sold" comparables, as the current listings might be pie in the sky.
- Get within plus or minus one bedroom and plus or minus one bath.
- Deduct for things like busy roads, lack of garage, weird layout, and so on.
- Use software such as Redfin (not Zillow because it doesn't pull actual sold comps) to look up comparable properties.
- Ideally, check in with a realtor in your area to verify what they think the property could sell for when you have it fixed up.

#2: DETERMINE REPAIR COSTS

There is software that gives you great estimates for repairs as you punch in what you plan to do with the property. There's even software that will connect with your local hardware store to give you a great idea of the approximate cost for the exact materials. When you get the property under contract, you're definitely going to want to have a contractor (or two or three) bid it out to get a more exact number. (For my up-to-date software recommendations, set up a call with me through www.lambertbonus.com.)

#3: RUN THE FORMULA

Now that you have those two key numbers, you're going to run this formula:

ARV (after repair value) × 0.75 (repair costs)

This formula takes into account making a 10 percent profit, as well as your selling and money costs (approximately 15 percent of the after-repair value). You'll want to carefully get all costs included before you finalize the purchase, but this formula will give you a rough estimate you can use to submit an initial offer.

FIVE STEPS TO ANALYZING A RENTAL

It's also important to do a lightning analysis when you're looking at a potential rental property (as opposed to a fix and flip). There are a few extra steps you need to do, and the formula is a bit different.

#1: DETERMINE THE VALUE

Start by determining the value of the property, following the same guidelines as for a fix and flip. It's important to consider the type of condition you're looking into. A rental doesn't need to be in as pristine condition as a flip. Keep that in mind.

#2: FACTOR MONTHLY PAYMENT

To calculate your mortgage payment, use a mortgage calculator app such as EZCalculators to get the principal and interest payment. Then look up and add the tax data by using Redfin. Add a bit for the going rate on insurance in your area as well. The full payment is often referred to as principal, interest, taxes, and insurance (PITI).

#3: DETERMINE AVERAGE GROSS RENT

To get a good starting place for rent, enter the property information into a site such as Rentometer. You'll want to get a more precise estimate from a property manager in your area before you finalize your purchase.

#4: DETERMINE GROSS CASH FLOW

To factor the gross cash flow, use the following formula:

Gross Rent – PITI = Gross Cash Flow

If you're in an appreciating market, like Utah, it's okay if your cash flow is a few hundred dollars, as you would likely make that up in appreciation. Yet if you're in a pretty stagnant real estate market, such as the Midwest, you're going to want a higher gross cash flow. There are a few other expenses to consider in the next section.

#5: FACTOR IN OTHER EXPENSES AND RUN THE FORMULA

Other expenses are important to factor in, such as property management (usually 10 percent of gross rent), vacancy (usually 10 percent of gross rent), and repairs and maintenance (usually 10 percent of gross rent). You may end up paying less than this, yet it's a good rule of thumb to factor in. Be conservative in your estimates, as it is better to make more than you expect rather than less. To estimate your expenses, use this formula:

Gross Rent × 0.3 = Expenses

You can then calculate your net monthly cash flow with this formula:

Gross Cash Flow − Expenses = Net Monthly Cash Flow

Alternatively, this equation calculates the same thing with fewer steps:

Gross Rent × 0.7 − PITI = Net Monthly Cash Flow

Following these five steps will give you a good sense of what you could expect to earn in cash flow on your deal.

KEY TAKEAWAYS

Deal analysis skills are vital for you to make money rather than lose it. You're going to be analyzing a lot of properties, though, so you can't afford to overanalyze deals either. By running some lightning formulas, you will be able to quickly arrive at a conclusion of what you can make as a preliminary offer. You can then tweak it later if you need to. You will want to run more detailed analyses before you actually buy a property. For free deal analysis tools, go to www.lambertbonus.com.

The next step, and the focus of the next chapter, is negotiating the deal.

TAKE ACTION EXERCISE:
LIGHTNING DEAL ANALYSIS

*(Download a printable version at
www.lambertbonus.com.)*

1. Write about one or two things you found most helpful in this chapter that you want to apply to your career.

2. Are you more interested in buying a flip or a rental?

3. If your analysis showed the after-repair value (ARV) is $200,000 and the repair costs are $30,000, what is your maximum allowable offer? Check your work at the end of the exercise.

4. Let's analyze your own residence address, imagining you were to rent it out. What would be your gross monthly cash flow using the formula above?

5. What would be your net cash flow on your residence after all your other expenses were factored in?

6. Would your residence make a good rental property? Why or why not?

*The answer to question 3 is $120,000, the maximum allowable offer ($200,000 × 0.75 - $30,000).

CHAPTER 13

NEGOTIATING THE DEAL

I get a high percentage of deals from my investor community. One day, Lani, a friend from my investor community in Las Vegas, gave me a call. She had a friend of a friend who was anxious to move and did not want to go through a realtor. I met with the sellers, a very nice elderly couple, and we hit it off. I asked about their family, where they were moving and why, and got to know them. I then took a look around the property and got a sense for what it might cost to fix it up. In discussing it with Lani, she told me my offer probably needed to come in at $230,000 to get the deal because someone else had offered them $225,000. I had the contract with me and started negotiations at $225,000. They hemmed and hawed, and I let them know if they would sign the contract tonight, I could go ahead and give them $230,000. We got under contract that night! (This is a good reminder to always come prepared with your contracts printed out and ready to be signed.)

The next week I brought a contractor in who was probably a bit of a perfectionist. He saw all kinds of red flags and told me it would take over $100,000 to fix it up. I wasn't sure how much I trusted his estimate, but I called another meeting with the sellers. I shared all of the contractor's concerns and told them I needed to buy the house for $200,000. They were a bit shocked and needed some time to think. The next morning, we signed an addendum reducing the price to $200,000!

The night after closing, a different contractor went over to scope out the property. He noticed a few signs that indicated the house had been a meth house. It just so happened that the title company hadn't yet gotten around to recording and funding the project. I called them up and let them know what had happened. I got in touch with the sellers and confronted them on the meth. They weren't happy at all, but with gentle language about informing the health department, they got on board for another $8,000 price reduction! As it turned out, the rehab only cost about $53,000, and the meth cost $4,000 to remediate. I went on to sell the house for $370,000 and pocketed nearly $80,000! This was my first fix and flip I had negotiated by myself.

Negotiating your target price and getting the contract signed are essential skills to develop. The aim of this chapter is to illustrate some key principles to negotiate the most profitable deal possible.

BUILDING RAPPORT

The most important step in the entire process is to build rapport and trust with the seller. It is not always easy to connect with a complete stranger, especially when they're in distress and in a very different situation from yourself. A core strategy is to move from less intrusive to more intrusive questions over the course of the conversation.

For example, you won't start out the conversation with a question like "How did you get so far behind on your mortgage?" Instead, you should start with questions like "I'm looking to buy a house in this neighborhood. What do you like best about living here? What do you dislike about it?" Get them to start describing what it's like and they'll open up. Then you can start moving into more intrusive questions about their situation. "Why would you want to move out of a beautiful home like this?" Be sure to show your desire to help.

The biggest key in building rapport is to talk as little as possible. Rather, you want to make statements like "Tell me more about that." Once they finish talking, you can dig deeper and get even more info. You'll be surprised how much they end up talking, because it's rare to find many people who actually listen. Let them talk as long as possible.

Be prepared for a variety of emotions. People in distressing situations need someone who is willing to listen to their distress with compassion.

WALK THROUGH THE HOUSE

Ask if they could show you the house. This is another chance to build rapport. Ask about family pictures, make observations, and give them compliments where you can. Definitely have a notepad and take notes on what needs to be fixed. Even better, ask permission to take a video of the house so you can review it later or send it to a contractor to get an estimate. Pay close attention to things like the foundation, roof, furnace, and air conditioner.

BECOME A P.I.G.

Take the pressure off yourself to be some all-star closing genius. Instead, see yourself as a P.I.G., a professional information gatherer. You want to leave the house with as clear a picture about their motive to sell as you can. You'll want to gather some specific numbers about what they think the house is worth, what interest rate they're paying, and what the mortgage balance is. I provide full scripts for my team members and role-play with them, so they know what to say and how to say it.

TALK THE SELLER THROUGH YOUR NUMBERS

Come into the appointment having printed off some comparable properties to show what the house could sell for. You will want to be conservative in the comparables you show, which is fair because you're taking on the risk. You need to be as conservative as you can, and who knows, maybe you won't be able to sell for higher than the lower comparables available.

Then ask what they think the property is worth. You'll be surprised that some people don't understand real estate. They may tell you the value they bought it for ten years ago. If so, go with that number. Other times, they will overestimate the value. In that case, show them some of the lower comparables in the area to get them to a reasonable price.

Next, talk through some of the costs and expenses you will need to incur to buy the property fast, like the costs of hard money and repairs. Emphasize that they won't have to do anything, and you will take the property in its current condition. You want to be conservative and estimate high on the repairs because, who knows, you may end up paying more than you think, and you almost always do. In addition to repair costs, let them know about the cost of hard money, private money, title insurance, and closing costs.

It's okay to let them know you don't work for free and you were hoping to make a bit as well. Consider telling them a conservative amount you want to make. You'll be surprised how relieved people are by this openness, and you even build rapport by telling them. Failing to admit that you're seeking a commission can feel like you're trying to con them.

The more you can walk them back through the numbers the better, so that when you get to your low price, they aren't completely shocked. They may have thought they could get more, but once you show them everything, it starts to make sense to them.

I also like to point out the alternative, which is selling through a realtor. Emphasize how, with a realtor, they will have to pay out of pocket to repair everything to get it ready to sell and how it costs about 10 percent of the value of the house to sell it. Also describe how 40 percent of deals with a realtor fall out of contract and have to start all over. Emphasize how it will take forever with a realtor, but with you, they'll get the money right away and you'll take the home in its current condition. I always come ready to make two different offers: one is cash now and one is *Subject To* the existing mortgage. You can offer them a bit more to do *Subject To* because that saves you on costs and gives you more options.

WALK THE SELLER THROUGH YOUR NUMBERS

CHECKLIST
- [ ] List of three comparable homes
- [ ] Hard money costs
- [ ] Private money costs
- [ ] Closing costs
- [ ] Repair costs
- [ ] Risk and your compensation (You've got to put food on the table, too!)

MONEY YOU SAVE THEM
- [ ] Realtor fees (Remember, 40 percent of realtor deals fall through.)
- [ ] Their time and time is money

CLOSE THE DEAL WITH INCENTIVES

Once you have presented their options to them (cash now or *Subject To* the existing mortgage), ask which offer they like better. Have the contract ready to sign with them, and if they start having concerns again, take the time to ask more questions. Find out their concerns and resolve them.

I usually go a little lower than I actually want in my initial offer, so I have some room for negotiation. If they seem close to moving forward but are asking for time to think about it, I'll offer them a couple thousand more for signing with me that day on the spot. If you absolutely can't get them to sign then, schedule a follow-up appointment to meet up and get the deal done then.

KEY TAKEAWAYS

Negotiating the deal is a vital step to buying a deal that will make you money. This is where you make money—when you buy, not when you sell. Build rapport from the beginning. Walk through the house. Gather information. Present how you arrived at your offer price. Then close the deal by giving a last-minute incentive. These steps will help you get more contracts signed by more sellers, which will make you more money.

Once you've secured your deal, your due diligence and work on the property begins. At this stage, it's critical to build a dream team of professionals. We'll look at how to do this in the next chapter.

TAKE ACTION EXERCISE: NEGOTIATING THE DEAL

(Download a printable version at www.lambertbonus.com.)

1. Write about one or two things you found most helpful in this chapter that you want to apply to your career.

2. What is your favorite way to build rapport with others?

3. List some questions you may ask a stranger to help them feel comfortable with you.

CHAPTER 14

BUILD YOUR DREAM TEAM

I bought one house *Subject To* and the house appreciated quite a bit. The original seller got greedy and came up with a plan to try to reclaim his property. Thankfully, someone at my title company tipped me off, and I was able to ambush that seller. I had an amazing hard money lender that paid off his loan before he could try anything. He got his full payday he was due, and I was able to stop his attempt to go back on our deal.

This story ends with me selling the property for $103,000 profit. I think back on what I would have done without certain key team members. If the person at my title company hadn't tipped me off, things could have turned out very differently. Additionally, this title company had also written the contracts in a way that was favorable to me, so I could pay off this seller without him even signing again. I also couldn't have pulled this deal off without a loyal hard money lender. He was willing to do a quick close within forty-eight hours of my request, which allowed me to blindside the seller to make sure he couldn't do anything sneaky.

Real estate investing is a team sport with many important players, and you are the head coach. In this chapter, I'll spell out the role of every team member and provide insight about how to build your real estate team, both offense and defense.

YOUR ROLE AS HEAD COACH

I'm a huge college football fan! At the biggest and best programs, the head football coach isn't in charge of all the drills and training; he has assistants cover most of that. So, then, what are the primary responsibilities of the head football coach?

1. **Recruit good talent.** A great coach must surround himself with incredible talent on both sides of the ball. Getting a phone call and being courted by the head coach is often what sways some of the best five-star athletes. One of your main jobs is recruiting good team members for your offense and defense.
2. **Line up great opportunities.** A head coach is often part

of the negotiations to schedule certain non-conference games. These games can often make or break whether the team goes to the college football playoff. In real estate, your job is to line up deals for your team to go to work on.

3. **Create a high-level strategy/game plan.** A head coach is also responsible for planning the strategy and game plan for the team. This is where you want to spend a lot of your time focusing on the big-picture plays for your business.

OFFENSE

Your offense is the part of the team that gets you deals, fixes them, and sells them, so you make money. These include contractors, lenders, wholesalers, realtors, and property managers.

CONTRACTORS

A contractor who does quality work at a quick pace and who is honest is worth his weight in gold. Ideally, you want someone with a general contractor's license who has a crew with subcontractors. These individuals can bust out every job you need without you having to do it all yourself. But if you want to save a little money, you can hire subcontractors yourself (or have an assistant do it). Then coordinate their efforts to get the jobs done quickly.

LENDERS

You're usually going to need a hard money lender and a private money lender for every deal. (In chapter 7, I discuss money lenders in a lot more detail.) You want individuals with competitive rates, who do not charge huge fees and high interest rates, and who can act quickly. Some deals you'll need to pay for with short notice, so your money lenders can be some of your most important players on the team.

WHOLESALERS

A wholesaler is a professional real estate investor specializing in massive marketing campaigns. They connect with a lot of potential sellers, and they get the property under contract. Next, they sell the contract to someone like me who flips the house. They don't ever even own the property or put any money on the deal. It's great to have several wholesalers on your team who are sending properties to you. That way you don't even have to find the deal yourself. If you enjoy finding deals, you may want to become a wholesaler, as you can make a great profit doing so.

REALTORS

Realtors can be of great benefit to investors. Not only can they handle all the paperwork for you when you buy and sell properties, but they can also find deals for you. Realtors have their eyes and ears to the ground, and I've bought many great deals from realtors. They get paid for doing all the paperwork on the deal they found for you. Oftentimes, you can negotiate a lower commission with the realtor than the typical 3 percent. Everyone wins.

PROPERTY MANAGERS

Before you can make any money on a rental, you're going to need a good property manager who will find you qualified tenants who can pay you every month. These professionals will help you determine what your house could rent for. They will market your property on many websites and screen every applicant. They will be a helpful buffer between you and your tenant to make hassle-free monthly checks.

DEFENSE

They say the best offense is a great defense. Typically, it's the team with the best defense who wins the national championships. It is no different in real estate. There are so many legal issues, and you can get creamed if you do things incorrectly. Some members of your defensive team include title officers, real estate attorneys, property insurance officers, accountants, and inspectors.

TITLE OFFICERS

The most important defense title companies offer you is a free and clear title. I've nearly purchased homes that would have been an awesome deal if it hadn't been for the $100,000-plus in liens on the property. How scary it would have been had I bought one of these. Don't mess around and fail to get something like title insurance. It is an important cost of doing business. My title companies have drafted much of my paperwork. They have provided educational mastermind opportunities, and given fantastic advice. I've had title companies even send me real estate deals, so there's that too. These guys can be your champions!

REAL ESTATE ATTORNEYS

Real estate attorneys reduce your liability by setting up LLCs and trusts for you, S corporations for your taxes, and much, much more. A good real estate attorney can also draft your closing documents and make sure you are crossing every "T" and dotting every "I." If it ever comes to a lawsuit, you can get a litigation attorney to represent you in court. It is definitely worth it to get a good one.

PROPERTY INSURANCE

Of course, a lot can happen to a property, including natural disasters, fire, massive tenant damage, flooding, and much more. You could lose your entire investment if not for property insurance. I recently rewatched my favorite movie, *The Greatest Showman*. It stood out to me how his circus burned down and it would have been the end of him if it weren't for his partner. In our day and age with property insurance, he would be able to get a massive upgrade on his facility at no extra cost if a fire raged. Insurance is there to protect you, and it is important that you get adequate coverage.

ACCOUNTANTS

A good accountant could pay for himself ten times over. I can't tell you how many hundreds of thousands of dollars I have saved by hiring an excellent accountant. Make sure you educate yourself about all the huge benefits you can get from the tax system as an investor, so you can choose an accountant who can help you realize all the options available to you. This incredible defense is giving me loads more for my offense. It feels like a lot of interceptions returned for touchdowns. Make sure you get a great accountant.

INSPECTOR

Finally, an important part of your due diligence is getting a good home inspector. A home inspector can test for a myriad of problems that, if identified before the purchase, can avoid a lot of headaches later on. Playing great defense here can be like a fumble recovery; you can use a good inspection as leverage to get the price down some more.

HOW TO BUILD YOUR DREAM TEAM

There are a lot of ways to build your team, and the very best way is through your real estate investing community. My investing community is so comprehensive that it's a one-stop shop. I found all my team members for offense and defense through my investing community. Plus, I see all these community members every week. This allows me to build close and tight friendships with my team members that go far beyond just business. It's partly why they go to bat for me when I need it.

The next best thing to a tight community like mine is to attend your local real estate investing club meetings. Whatever you do, don't leave when the instruction ends. That's when the most valuable part of the meeting begins. Instead, network, network, network. Add people to your phone contacts and try them out next time you need X, Y, or Z. Make note of who is working well for your team and who you don't want to do repeat business with. As mentioned in chapter 5, you should have a spreadsheet to track your real estate team. (For a free spreadsheet download, visit www. lambertbonus.com.)

Another source for building your team is to ask your community or friends on social media for referrals. Most people won't suggest someone they're not sure about recommending, so it's a great way to put your team together.

KEY TAKEAWAYS

Putting together a first-rate real estate investing team is supremely important. They will make or break your pocketbook. Rather than a player on the field, view yourself as the head coach. Actively recruit great talent, and this will save you from having to do most of the heavy lifting. Offensive stars like contractors, lenders, wholesalers, realtors, and property managers are vital for finding and processing your deals. You'll also need a good defense, including title officers, attorneys, insurance officers, accountants, and inspectors. Your best people will come from referrals, which you can get from your investor community, real estate clubs, and social media. You can only grow as good as the team you surround yourself with.

With a great team in place, you can begin executing deals, and then you can turn your sights to building and protecting your empire, which is the focus of the next part of the book.

TAKE ACTION EXERCISE:
YOUR REAL ESTATE TEAM

*(Download a printable version at
www.lambertbonus.com.)*

1. Write about one or two things you found most helpful
   in this chapter that you want to apply to your career.

2. Whom do you know who could be part of your team?

3. Whom do you know who could refer you to people to
   add to your team?

4. What networking meetings are available in your area
   so you can start connecting with potential team members?

PART IV

BUILDING
AND
PROTECTING

CHAPTER 15

NAIL IT AND THEN SCALE IT

For a while, I was doing a maximum of about three fix and flips at a time. I thought this was all I could do, but then I realized I was simply being held back by some limiting beliefs. I decided to work to change that belief system and was able to secure about $600,000 in private money at a good interest rate. Suddenly, I was on fire. Within a few months, I ramped up to fourteen deals at a time, and I made more in real estate than I ever had before. It was *so* invigorating!

Once you nail the process, it is time to scale your business by creating systems and learning how to further delegate to your team. The goal of this chapter is to show you some systems you can use to scale your business and to build an empire.

SNOW FORT PRINCIPLE: MANAGING SEVERAL ONGOING PROJECTS

It snowed every winter where I grew up in the Rocky Mountain West. Every time the snow fell, my brothers and I eagerly put on our warm clothes and headed outside to make snow forts. Now, a good snow fort requires a series of large snowballs, and we would often have several snowballs going at once. Having many snowballs in the works was more efficient and would give us a needed break when one snowball was getting very large. Sometimes we'd roll one snowball for a while, get bored of it, start a new one, and then come back to the old one. Once we got a snowball to a rollable size, we'd call one or two others to help us push the snowball until we got it to the right size. Then we'd line them up and stack them on top of each other. Oftentimes, we'd even make two forts at once, for later snowball fights.

In this analogy, each snowball represents a house project. Each snowball is a different size, and you're constantly pushing and building several snowballs at once. At a certain point in the process, you will call in other partners to help push and enlarge the snowball, preparing it to contribute to the fort of your wealth. When you have different house projects going at different stages, you can keep all your team members engaged. This way, nobody gets too overwhelmed.

PROJECT PROGRESSION CHART

When you have several projects going on at the same time, all at different stages, it's critical to stay organized. A project progression chart is key.

Create a spreadsheet that has three main columns to track all your deals. Put them into the categories of Under Contract/Purchasing, Fixing, or Selling/Renting. Then list all the properties you have in the hopper at each stage. Include a goal date to get each property to the next phase and a column that has the to-dos for each property to get them to the next phase.

ADDRESS	UNDER CONTRACT/ PURCHASING	FIXING	SELLING/ RENTING
123 W. Sunflower Dr.	X	X	X
756 E. Rolling Hills Dr.	X		
3459 Horseshoe Bend Ave.	X	X	

RULE OF THREE

You want to start out having at least one deal in every phase of the process. This will help you create a reliable stream of constant income. Instead of selling all your properties at once, you will have a steady flow of sales. It also helps because you won't bury the people on your team and will instead give them a more even flow of work.

As you scale up your business, try to get two properties in each phase, then three, and so on. By staggering projects, you can make things easier on yourself. Of course, things are not always going to work out smoothly. Sometimes projects move more quickly or slowly than you expect, so be prepared for occasional crunch times. The most stressed I have ever been was when I had six properties selling at the same time, and I was running like a chicken with his head cut off. It all worked out with sweet payouts in the end!

DELEGATE TO PROJECT MANAGERS

As you look at your project progression chart, write down all the to-dos that need to be done for each project. Add yet another column labeled Assigned To and then try to delegate most if not all the tasks to either a project manager or an assistant. The more you can delegate, the faster you'll fill your pipelines, and the more money you're going to make. Review chapter 4 for inspiration on delegating tasks.

DELEGATE TO PARTNERS

If your business plan includes partners, try to delegate to your partners as much as you can. Most of them will appreciate the learning opportunities. I have a team of five assistants, but they are all part time, because I delegate so many responsibilities to my partners. Most of my partners are still in the "nail it" stage, where they need to learn how it all works before they can move forward to the "scale it" stage. Usually, by the time they hit the "scale it" stage, they are independent and seeking "nail it" partners of their own, whom they can empower.

KEY TAKEAWAYS

To build an empire, you must expand by working on multiple projects simultaneously. Get organized by creating a spreadsheet of all your properties at each of the three phases and then shoot to have at least one property in each of the three phases. To handle everything, you'll need to delegate both to project managers and to partners. Otherwise, you'll be stuck doing everything yourself, and you won't be able to create a sustainable business.

As you scale and grow, you'll be making more money, but much of it will be tied up in nonliquid assets. This can be a problem if you hit a cash crunch, so in the next chapter, we'll look at a great strategy for building liquid reserves—cash value life insurance.

CHAPTER 16

BE YOUR OWN BANK

A few years ago, I had somewhat of a financial crisis. For a few months straight, my business expenses were so high and my revenue so low that I hit a serious cash crunch and began to panic. It paralyzed me like nothing I have experienced, and the fear and dread inside me killed my confidence, making it even harder to produce revenue. I started preparing for the worst.

Fortunately, I pushed through this financial crisis and pulled out. Yet a month's worth of panic attacks were so painful that I vowed never to experience this again!

Real estate is the *best* possible investment, but it does have maybe one weakness: it lacks liquidity. Oftentimes, you need to put more money in and wait for something to sell. Many times the best-case scenario to get your money out is two months, with four to five months being the average. If you experience some crisis in your life, you may not be able to wait ten days, let alone four to five months, to cover it. That's exactly why it's important to have liquid reserves. Also, during a down market, the last thing you want to do is be forced to sell a rental property for a loss because you didn't have the money available to sustain it.

This issue of liquidity is exactly the problem I faced. I had plenty of real estate assets, but they were not very liquid. What I needed were liquid reserves. My reserve account had to be pretty massive—enough to give me the liquidity I might need to float fifty-plus rental properties. I wanted something that could make me money while it was sitting but that was also resistant to downturns in the market, since it was during downturns when I'd need it most. After a lot of research, I ended up finding the solution through a cash value life insurance policy.

THE SECURITY BUCKET: CASH VALUE LIFE INSURANCE

Tony Robbins suggests you put your money in three buckets—a security bucket, an investment bucket, and a dream bucket. It's easy to put money in the fun dream bucket to buy cars, nice homes, and trips. The investment bucket is sexy, and you're reading this book because you love the high-return investment bucket.

Then there's the security bucket. It doesn't make a fantastic return, but it's going to cover your butt when the market turns. It's exactly what's going to ensure you don't lose all your wealth during a bad time. The security bucket might be the most important of all three. Not having it could cause an utter disappearance of the other two buckets you have worked so hard to build.

A cash value life insurance policy functions as your security bucket. Life insurance companies are also investment companies. When you make your initial payment and your premium payment, they take that money and invest it for high returns. In exchange, they are willing to both give you a death benefit and share some of their investing profits with you. In this way, the right life insurance policy allows you to create a family legacy and reserves for your business, and it also lets you become your own bank.

MAKE SAFE MONEY WHILE BUILDING RESERVES

One of the best parts about using life insurance is that these reserve funds are completely insulated from market losses. Chances are you're more likely to need the money in a down market than when things are hot. The last thing you want is to have your money invested in securities and then to have your reserves go up in smoke.

With life insurance, you can never lose money, as the

growth is protected from losses. There's what's called a floor, and the company won't let the money go below zero. It's completely recession-proof, making it as safe as it can get. With an indexed universal life policy, you can earn 12 to 13 percent during the good years and lose nothing during the bad years.

Here's something that happened to me, to illustrate this principle. Over a few years, I invested a few hundred thousand into indexed universal life. I also invested $40,000 into some bonds to diversify a bit. When COVID-19 roiled the security markets, I lost $25,000, or 62 percent of my bond option investment. Meanwhile, the hundreds of thousands I put in life insurance didn't lose a single penny!

I haven't had to dip into my reserves yet. But, during uncertain times, it gives me a lot of peace of mind knowing these reserves are protected from whatever happens in the market.

Another great benefit of using a life insurance policy for your reserves is that the growth is tax-free! That's right; you don't get taxed on the dividend earnings. You can just keep borrowing from it without getting taxed. Thus, you can move money around without worries of Uncle Sam getting a slice of the pie. This is appealing to those who crush it in real estate and make a lot of money. I know I personally love capturing market gains tax-free.

PROVIDE A SECURITY NET FOR YOUR FAMILY

With a cash value life insurance policy, not only can you build liquid reserves, you can also make decent returns and provide a safety net for your family. You can get a large death benefit so that if anything happens, your spouse and kids are set for life. I obtained a $10 million policy on myself, and I've noticed my wife no longer reminds me to buckle my seat belt. In fact, when I told her I wanted to go skydiving in Hawaii, she suggested I should try it a couple of times if I liked it!

All joking aside, this is a huge safety net for my family. My dad died an early death at fifty-seven from cancer. He had the foresight to invest a lot of money in life insurance, and as a result, my mom is completely taken care of for the rest of her life.

Even not considering the death benefit, the reserves themselves are a great safety net. I just sent a check to my life insurance reserve policy, bringing my total to $500,000 in liquid reserves! In case of rainy days, I now have enough in reserves to live comfortably without income for over five years!

BE YOUR OWN BANK

Another reason why life insurance is the perfect complement to real estate investing is because you can be your own bank and fund deals out of your policy. I bought my first flip with a loan from my life insurance policy!

More recently, when we moved into our dream house, I had to initially put 20 percent down, which was $220,000. I was so grateful I had been putting so much money away in my policy. It made it possible for me to take a loan for the full amount so I could make the most important purchase of my life. The story has such a happy ending, as I was able to add a sports court at my new home just in time for the HELOC appraisal. This made the value come in at $200,000 higher than I had paid to purchase it. With the sale of my old home, I was able to get all the down payment money back, plus an additional $40,000, which I used to pay back the life insurance loan right away. Talk about being your own bank!

As another example, I recently wrote a check for $139,000 to one of my life insurance companies to max fund it for the fourth year in a row. I then immediately borrowed $120,000 back. I love it because I'll make about a 9 percent return on the $139,000, and I'll then pay 4.5 percent interest on the $120,000 loan. I'm making a 4.5 percent return on the $120,000 that I'm now using for other purposes.

KEY TAKEAWAYS

Cash value life insurance can be the ultimate complement to your real estate investing. Insurance can provide you with reserves that get you a good return but will never lose. You can borrow from your life insurance to do more deals. It provides security for your family should something ever happen to you, and the growth came to you tax-free. Hard to beat this instrument!

Speaking of taxes, in the next chapter, we'll look at some other strategies for saving on taxes.

TAKE ACTION EXERCISE:
CASH VALUE LIFE INSURANCE

(Download a printable version at
www.lambertbonus.com.)

1. Write about one or two things you found most helpful in this chapter that you want to apply to your career.

2. What's most appealing to you about the Be Your Own Bank strategy?

3. What kind of death benefit would you want for your spouse/kids or future spouse/kids?

4. With a minimum of $5,000 to $10,000 per rental in reserves, how much will you need in reserves (based on the number of properties needed to hit your financial independence goal)?

CHAPTER 17

SAVE ON TAXES

My friend did better than ever financially last year. He found a solution that allowed him to write off most of his income but also allowed him to qualify for all the loans he applied for. It's like having your cake and eating it too. With this one strategy, my friend was able to write off $320,000 and ended up getting a $3,500 refund check while still qualifying for a home loan for over $1 million!

As you begin to create massive wealth, you must learn to preserve it from being taken by Uncle Sam. The aim of the current chapter is to give you an overview of some of the amazing ways you can save big-time on your taxes. All of this is done in a way that is legal, moral, and ethical. Remember, I am not an accountant, and some of these tax laws may have changed, so please consult your accountant before taking action. These are some of the best ways I have found to save on my taxes.

START A REAL ESTATE BUSINESS

One of the best ways to save on taxes when your real estate business starts making at least $30,000 a year is to form an S corporation. An S corporation allows you to avoid having to pay hefty self-employment taxes. If you're still working a W-2 job, you can write off not only business expenses but also the income from your W-2 salary, a total game changer for a lot of people.

PAY YOUR KIDS

If you have children, you can pay each child up to $12,000 a year for working in your business, and it's a tax write-off for you. They should be old enough that it passes the smell test of actually being able to do something. It's a double bonus because you can teach your children work ethic, get them involved in the family business, and teach them how money works. For instance, my oldest son, Hyrum, works for me, and he pays all my bills, fixes things on my computer, and even runs numbers for deals. I will often take my other children to a fix-and-flip property right before I put it on the market to do some yard work. They pick up any garbage so the house looks great. Instead of having your children work for minimum wage, why not have them help you in your business and pay them well for their participation? It's a win for everyone!

RETIREMENT ACCOUNTS

Retirement accounts can be an absolute game changer for tax savings. There are several different write-offs you can get now, including long-term write-offs if you do deals within your retirement account. If you want to go this route, you will need to learn all the rules and regulations for using your retirement account so you do not get into trouble.

SELF-DIRECTED IRA

At the time of this writing, you can contribute $5,500 per spouse or $11,000 for a family to an annual, self-directed IRA. This means you can get up to an $11,000 write-off. Or you can make it a Roth IRA and pay some taxes up front. With this method, you can then conduct real estate deals through the Roth IRA account without paying taxes.

SOLO 401(K)

You can self-direct your 401(k) if it's not invested by your current company. You can learn how to roll it over to become self-directed. If you make a high income, you could contribute as much as $56,000 and your spouse could also contribute $56,000. That's a total of $112,000 in retirement account money. You are able to either get an immediate write-off from this, or you can turn the account into a Roth and you'll avoid paying taxes on all the deals you do within it. It's a process that feels magical and allows for peace of mind.

DEPRECIATION AND COST SEGREGATION

Perhaps the most powerful strategy is depreciation and cost segregation. This strategy can only be employed by individuals who spend at least 750 hours a year (fourteen hours a week) in real estate or trade businesses.

Here's an example of how this strategy works. Let's say you find and buy a rental for $400,000. You can then have a study conducted on that rental that segregates five-year, seven-year, and fifteen-year assets, based on how long it takes for those assets to wear out. For example, five- and seven-year assets might include paint, carpet, some of the plumbing, some of the electrical, and so on. Anything that can be classified in one of these categories can qualify for a bonus, and you can take all the depreciation as a bonus in year one. What this equates to is that ultimately about 25 percent of the purchase price of a rental can be written off in the year it is rented out. In this scenario, you can get a $100,000 write-off. A friend of mine wrote off as much as $320,000.

One of the most powerful aspects of this strategy is that typically writing off all your income disqualifies you for bank loans, but this is not the case with cost segregation! They actually count the amount you segregated toward your total income. Thus, despite a $320,000 write-off, my friend was able to qualify for a $1 million mortgage for his dream home!

KEY TAKEAWAYS

Real estate investors get so many perks and can often write off most of what they make. You can creatively take advantage of tax-saving strategies such as forming an S corporation and paying your children. You can also set up retirement accounts and cost segregate your properties. These and many more strategies could really save you from major hurt during tax season.

In the next chapter, we'll look at the final strategy for building and protecting your empire: how to thrive in a down market.

TAKE ACTION EXERCISE:
TAX SAVINGS

(Download a printable version at
www.lambertbonus.com.)

1. Write about one or two things you found most helpful in this chapter that you want to apply to your career.

2. What tax-saving strategy seems the most accessible for you to apply right away?

3. What strategy do you think would give you the most benefit?

4. What will you call your real estate business entity?

CHAPTER 18

HOW TO THRIVE IN A DOWN MARKET

Tony was aggressive and so anxious to buy property that he used about every penny he had to buy more. He drew down every credit line and maxed out every credit card. His philosophy was to go big or go home, and he was going to make it happen. He acquired twenty rental properties. Six of them didn't produce cash flow, but he figured it was still worth it, due to the appreciating market. He also had ten flips going and didn't have any other exit plan in mind if the market shifted.

When a huge global recession hit the market, Tony was in a world of hurt. At first, his tenants continued to pay rent, but when several of them lost their jobs, they stopped paying rent, and he started losing the cash flow. The roof on one rental went bad, and he didn't have the funds to fix it. The tenant moved out. Another house had a sewer issue, and again, there were no funds to take care of it. Without reserves, Tony had no choice but to let the house with the roof problem go into foreclosure. The house with the sewer problem and the six properties without cash flow were next to go into foreclosure. He also lost three rentals where the tenants had stopped paying rent. For these properties, all the equity he'd accumulated now went to the highest bidder at the auction. This was his worst nightmare, and unfortunately, it got worse.

When the values of the properties went down, Tony was unwilling to lower the prices. He was stuck on getting the value he initially planned for, so he kept the prices high for too long. Finally, when he saw the writing on the wall, he lowered the prices, but by then the market had slipped even further. Soon, all the profit was gone from his deals, and he had to have a tough conversation with his money lenders, who would need to foreclose on him. Several lenders and partners filed lawsuits. Tony had to declare bankruptcy and lost the rest of his properties and all the goodwill relationships he'd developed.

* * *

Tina was also very excited to get a lot of properties and to make it work, but she built a bit more cautiously. Instead of using every penny to buy the next property, she made sure to have a minimum of $8,000 in reserves for each of her fifteen rentals. In addition, Tina had a few hundred thousand in reserves in her cash value life insurance policy that she could borrow from at any time. She made sure every property provided at least a few hundred dollars in cash flow a month. She also had ten flips going on.

When the global recession hit, she did a careful analysis of all her properties. She decided to sell two of her lower-performing rentals and added a huge sum of money to her reserves. She did a rental analysis on all her flips and found four of them looked like they would provide good cash flow as rentals. She immediately began reaching out to her contacts to see who might be interested in being a credit partner so she could get rid of the hard money lender. This way, she would retain a 50 percent share of the equity in the deals and more than replace the rental income that she lost with the sale of the lower-performing rentals. Just like Tony, some of her tenants stopped making payments, and she had a roof issue and sewer issue, but she was able to afford the repairs and easily weather the storm with her reserves. As such, she didn't have to sell any of her remaining rentals.

She kept a close finger on the pulse of the market, often getting advice from her realtor friends about what was going on. She made sure that she stayed ahead of the market and was able to sell every one of her remaining six flips by lowering the prices. She made close to half of her initial projected profit on five of the flips and only took a loss (of $5,000) on one of them. Then, when she felt like the market had bottomed out, she used the cash she'd made from the sale of her two rentals to buy another six deeply discounted rentals. She had gained everyone's trust and several people were happy to be her money partner. Over the next year, she was able to buy an additional eight rentals, bringing her total to thirty-six.

Since so many people had lost their houses and there was crazy demand for rentals, Tina's cash flow increased quite a bit. All the money the government printed to help everyone survive the recession inflated the dollar more than in recent decades. As a result, the value of mortgages had decreased considerably, wages went up, and Tina was able to raise her rents. When the market rebounded, Tina sold sixteen of her rentals at high prices and was able to use that money to pay off the mortgages on her remaining twenty properties. Tina had certainly made the most of this economic recession and had come out *much* stronger as a result. She had succeeded where Tony failed because she was flexible and ready to pivot as needed, got help from partners, and had the reserves she needed to weather the storm.

SITUATIONAL ANALYSIS

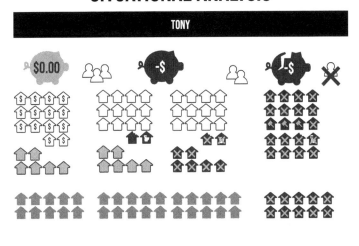

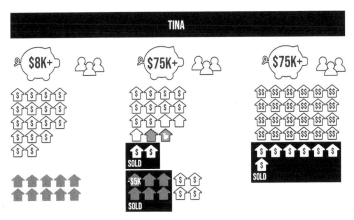

As long as you haven't overleveraged, down markets are the best time to find profitable real estate and inexpensive financing. My aim in this chapter is to illustrate both how to protect yourself in a down market and how to make the most of such conditions to ramp up your portfolio.

HOW TO PROTECT YOURSELF IN A DOWN MARKET

There are a few key principles you will need to follow to protect yourself from loss during a down market. These include building reserves and being willing to pivot with multiple exit strategies. Finally, stay ahead of the market by being aggressive with price reductions for flips.

RESERVES

The most important principle to maintain your assets is to have plenty of money in reserves so you can weather the storms that might come up. The last thing you want to do during a downturn is to have to sell a property at a loss. This is especially true for rental properties, because you should get higher rents in a downturn due to more demand (though you may also need to deal with tenants who can't pay their rent). You need enough reserves for each rental property to cover several months of vacancy, maintenance, and repairs. If so, you should be able to make it through until the market values recover. I recommend $5,000 to $10,000 per property, depending on the size of the home. As you get more properties, you should increase your reserves accordingly, as you now have more exposure.

PIVOTS AND EXIT STRATEGIES

It is important to be willing to pivot on properties when economic turbulence comes. For example, during the last economic downturn, I had one property I had planned on renting out on a vacation rental site. Instead, I decided to sell the property and get the cash. I had a rental that was not performing, and I sold the home quickly in order to increase my cash reserves.

During economic downturns, you want to have multiple exit strategies. For instance, if I am going to flip a property, I will also do a rental analysis on it. That way, if the market goes down while I'm in the middle of the flip, I can turn around and rent it out with a credit partner and be just fine. Having multiple exit strategies keeps you safe during times of economic uncertainty.

STAY AHEAD OF THE MARKET WITH FLIPS

One Achilles' heel that can bite investors is chasing down the market instead of staying ahead of it. In other words, if the market starts to go down, they get stubborn and leave their property listed at a higher price for too long. By the time they finally drop the price, the market has gone even further down. They moved too slowly and ended up losing money they didn't have to lose; if only they had acted more quickly and aggressively in their price reductions.

TIME OF GREAT OPPORTUNITY

Around half of Fortune 500 companies started during the

Great Recession of 2008. The only time when more millionaires were made than the '08 recession was the Great Depression. Times of economic downturn are huge for investors, especially real estate investors. Why? Big problems require big problem-solvers. Also, shelter is essential and hard assets are king.

Here is my top-ten list for why economic downturns are the perfect time to invest in real estate:

1. Luxury industries such as travel, events, and entertainment often drop during down markets. In contrast, life essentials, such as shelter and food, are going to be more important during all down times, and people are always moving.
2. Big discounts come during down markets. The best time to buy Valentine's Day candy at a discount is not on February 13 or 14, but on February 15. Downturns are February 15 for real estate.
3. During a down real estate market, you keep getting monthly checks from your rentals.
4. Rental payments are the first check someone writes and the last one they skip. Everyone needs a place to live.
5. Money is cheap during down markets, with lower interest rates for mortgages, private money, and so on.
6. The nonprofessional investors are scared away in a downturn, so there are more deals for the professionals.
7. Divorce goes up quite a bit when the market turns,

and this creates more motivated sellers who need to urgently sell their house.

8. Defaults go up in a downturn. People lose their houses left and right, need cash, and are in need of creative solutions. If you know a lot about *Subject To*, you can help a lot of people.

9. People tend to switch jobs more often during down markets, and so displacement is rampant. The need for real estate professionals with creative solutions is higher.

10. Demand for rentals goes up in a bad economy, because so many people are losing their homes and need to move into a rental. This typically makes rents go up!

Prepare yourself for the next downturn so you will be able to help more people than ever before!

INFLATION CAN BE YOUR ALLY

We tend to look at inflation as a bad thing, but if you own a lot of properties, inflation (which often happens during a downturn) can be your friend! Let me illustrate why that may be.

Let's say you own a house that you bought at market value for $300,000. It rents for $2,000, and the monthly payment is $1,500. Therefore, the cash flow is $500.

Now, serious inflation kicks in and the mortgage is worth

comparatively less money than it was before inflation. Since people are also getting higher salaries from inflation, you can now rent the place for $3,000, increasing your cash flow to $1,500! You can now pay off that mortgage much faster, and the debt is worth a lot less, which helps you out in significant ways. Now imagine if you had fifty-plus properties when the market corrected. Due to inflation, that could be some amazing benefits for you. This is the power of hard assets.

KEY TAKEAWAYS

Down markets will happen, as we're constantly in a state of flux with the economy. You can protect yourself from the down market by having plenty of reserves. Pivots and exit strategies are also crucial. Do not chase down the market in selling a property, but be willing to be aggressive in price reductions. Keep in mind the many great reasons to invest during a down market and how even inflation can help you. There is no reason not to take action; just be cautious.

Now that you have tips and strategies for building and protecting your empire, in the final part of the book, we'll look at some common psychological and emotional challenges you'll face in your career and how a success mindset can help you overcome them.

**TAKE ACTION EXERCISE:
THRIVING IN A DOWNTURN**

*(Download a printable version at
www.lambertbonus.com.)*

1. Write about one or two things you found most helpful in this chapter that you want to apply to your career.

2. What's the biggest economic crisis you have lived through?

3. What did you observe about real estate prices during that period?

4. Where do you see yourself storing your biggest source of reserves?

PART V

A SUCCESS MINDSET

CHAPTER 19

READY, FIRE, AIM

Tim was a great learner. When I presented him with a library of educational classes, he jumped on it. I have never seen someone listen to more classes. He was incredibly disciplined at listening and learning. Unfortunately, when it came to taking action, he never seemed to get around to it. When he would see a deal that looked promising, instead of jumping on it, he overanalyzed it. Either he talked himself out of it or someone else got the seller to sign on the dotted line before he could get to them. He eventually decided that real estate wasn't for him after all, and he soon forgot most of what he'd learned because he never applied it.

* * *

Alan also watched classes and educated himself, but he was a man of action. He was constantly analyzing deals and making offers. He would do a quick analysis before making an offer and then tie up the property. At that point, he would do his extensive due diligence before purchasing the property. Some properties weren't a good enough deal. He would first try to renegotiate, often using an inspection report to gain leverage. Many times it worked, but when he couldn't get it for what he needed to, he would just get his refundable earnest money deposit back and go look for the next property. His action mentality led him to do fifteen deals in his first year, which made him $250,000!

The people in both of these examples are members of my elite investing team. What held Tim up was *analysis paralysis*. He was afraid to take action because of the unknown. What if it was not a good deal? What if he lost money? What if, what if? These kinds of worries often paralyze even the best-intended investors into a state of inaction.

Clearly, the only way to make money in this business is by buying real estate. Unfortunately, Tim represents a lot of individuals I have coached, and many people are always "getting ready to get ready." Approaching deals like Alan— getting the deal under contract before doing the intense analysis—will generate far more deals for your business. The aim of this chapter is to encourage you to take massive action backed by caution in a Ready, Fire, Aim approach.

THE NEED FOR MASSIVE ACTION

"Action is the antidote to despair," said Joan Baez. You gain so much momentum by taking action! There's a certain energy and enthusiasm associated with taking action that propels you into more action. Believe me, once you get your first taste of success, you're going to want more of it!

The problem is that fear often holds people back from action. It's the first deal that's the hardest to do, and you just can't let yourself get cold feet. "Pushing through fear is less frightening than living with it and its associated helplessness. Feel the fear and do it anyway," said Susan Jeffers. Let that fear just flow through you. Don't let it paralyze you into inaction.

I know that's easier said than done, which is where the Ready, Fire, Aim strategy comes in handy.

READY, FIRE, AIM

I'm quite certain you have heard the phrase Ready, Aim, Fire before, but have you ever heard of Ready, Fire, Aim? This is a pretty incredible strategy for taking action but doing it in a cautious way to ensure you make a good profit. Here are the steps:

Ready. You need to be looking at potential deals constantly. When you see one that looks like an option, do the quick flip or rental analysis as discussed in chapter 12.

Fire. Now for the step that seems out of order. I say fire is step two because once your quick analysis suggests it could be a deal, you need to take action. Do whatever you can to get the property under contract at a price that is at least somewhat close to your quick projection. It is important that the seller signs the documents. This way, they can't sell the property to anyone else unless your contract with them expires or is voided. You have got the property locked up and it's practically yours for the taking. This is the step where fear becomes a problem, so remind yourself that you'll have a chance to do a thorough analysis after you fire. That really helps you to just get off your couch and do it.

Aim. Now that you've locked up the deal, you have given yourself time to do more serious due diligence without losing the deal to someone else. It also gives you a lot of negotiating power to drop the price if your inspection pulls up anything that isn't favorable (and it always will). I discuss the type of due diligence you'll want to be sure to do in more depth in the chapter on common pitfalls, chapter 21.

PRO TIP: WORK DOWN THE PRICE

You can get a property under contract at a price that isn't good enough for your numbers, because you can get them to drop their price later. You will get an inspection report that shows some of the problems. The idea is to show them or email them the report and to make a big deal of all the things that are wrong with the property. The great thing about getting a property under contract is that the seller has started counting their money. The seller feels relieved about this headache being taken away. Sellers often become pretty committed to the sale, to the point that you can often get them to go along with a price reduction. Your job is to excel at justifying it and pointing out how future buyers won't be happy with X, Y, or Z.

KEY TAKEAWAYS

Ready, Fire, Aim is a strategy that will get you into multiple deals because you won't get stuck in analysis-paralysis mode. Remind yourself that you can get your earnest money back for almost any reason. You have nothing to lose by getting a property under contract and then doing your due diligence afterward. You won't execute on each one you pick up, and using this safe method can help you release your inhibitions to pounce on more deals that will make you money!

In the next chapter, we'll look at another major fear people have—the fear of rejection—and how to overcome it.

TAKE ACTION EXERCISE:
READY, FIRE, AIM

*(Download a printable version at
www.lambertbonus.com.)*

1. Write about one or two things you found most helpful in this chapter that you want to apply to your career.

2. What do you see as some of the primary advantages to the Ready, Fire, Aim strategy?

3. How would you rate yourself on a scale from one (over-analyzer) to ten (extreme action-taker)?

4. If low on that scale, how will you overcome this tendency or push yourself toward greater action?

CHAPTER 20

OVERCOME REJECTION

What is the most important key to success? Intelligence? Nope. Hard work? Nope. The most important factor in success that separates the winners from the losers is how you deal with rejection and failure!

Those who have followed all the success I've had in real estate investing don't realize how much failure I endured before reaching financial independence. I help people have success a lot faster than I experienced. Here's a quick recap of my failed attempts over four years to find my first deal:

#1: I paid for a turnkey rental program. While they found me a rental, I failed to find anything myself and wasn't able to do another one.

#2: I paid for education with a guru and failed.

#3: I joined the local real estate investment clubs and failed.

#4: I quit my full-time job to do real estate full time (given my track record, crazy, right?) and made zero income for many months—a failure.

#5: I paid for personal coaching and failed.

#6: I spent 120 hours getting my realtor license and then failed.

#7: I connected with an amazing investor community, but my initial attempts still failed.

#8: I thought I could do real estate from Fiji and failed big-time, and came back to the United States.

What kept me going during four years of repeated failures? A powerful vision of financial independence through real estate investing. It is a journey. We all have our individual mindset barriers to overcome and skillsets to build. I began with few skills and a poor man's mindset, and this could not be overcome overnight. If you ever feel discouraged and wonder why it's not happening for you faster, remember, it took me four years of persistent action to get my first real deal. Having gone through all this, one goal of my book is to help you to experience far fewer pitfalls and struggles than I had, but failure is still part of the process. When you're knocked down, recommit and get back on your feet. Financial independence may be closer than you realize. You've got this! Rejection is perhaps the fiercest enemy of the investor, but you can overcome it!

Billionaire life coach and motivational speaker Tony Robbins once described what he saw as the key to success in life. He said, "The key to success in life, the key to wealth and happiness, is called achieving massive amounts of... rejection." Interesting, why would that be the case? He went on to explain, "The more rejection you get, the more acceptances and success you'll receive." To have success, you first have to try to put yourself out there.

A core problem with rejection is that it can be so debilitating for people. They will not try again. If you never try, you will never know if you could have succeeded. That is partly why fear of rejection and how you deal with rejection are two of the most reliable predictors of your ultimate success as an investor.

FEAR OF REJECTION IMPEDES YOUR PRODUCTIVITY

Fear of rejection will significantly harm your productivity as an investor. Fear of rejection tells you, "don't talk to sellers," "don't make offers," and "don't follow up with sellers"—three of the most important things you must do!

FEAR SAYS: DON'T TALK TO SELLERS

It takes a lot of guts to have a conversation with a seller, knowing there's a high probability you will be rejected and they won't sell you their house. I have known so many people who take an unnecessary amount of time getting ready to get ready. They don't take the plunge. They don't have conversations with the seller. I think the fear of rejection underlies much of why people do not even have a conversation.

FEAR SAYS: DON'T MAKE OFFERS

Fear also stops investors from making offers. Investors fear their offer will be rejected, so they don't even bother to submit it. It's like they look at the rejection of their offer as a rejection of themselves.

Believe me, this fear of rejection affects every field. As a professor, I spoke to a journal editor who had just received a "promotion" to become an editor at the top journal in the field of psychology. "Wow, I bet you're going to be extremely busy now?" I inquired, assuming his workload was going to be much heavier. "Actually, my editorial load will be significantly lighter at this journal," he replied.

"They only have about half the submissions as the journal I edited for previously." Initially, I found it surprising. The top journal would receive half the quantity of submissions as did the less prestigious journal. However, it makes perfect sense to me now—people fear and dread rejection at highly ranked journals. They prefer the reduced risk of submitting to lower ranked, less prestigious journals. How many of these articles that were never submitted could have been accepted at the top journal? We'll never know.

You miss every shot you don't take. So many sellers would take lower offers, but investors will never know because they fear making the offer in the first place.

FEAR SAYS: DON'T FOLLOW UP WITH SELLERS

Once an investor has been "rejected" by a seller, they can fear following up with that individual later on. In getting real estate deals, timing is everything. A seller who told you no a month ago may have just gotten a threatening letter from their bank. Now they are ready to sell, but you lost the opportunity because you were afraid they'd turn you down again if you were to approach them. I can't tell you how many deals have come to me when I followed up and reconnected with people who told me no the first time.

DEALING WITH REJECTION

Earl Graves said, "We keep going back, stronger, not weaker, because we will not allow rejection to beat us down. It will only strengthen our resolve. To be successful there is no other way." The truly successful investors strengthen their resolve when they receive rejection. Anyone can deal well with good fortune, but the true test of an individual is how he or she gets up after being knocked down. You can either become better or bitter. Here are some suggestions that may help after receiving those inevitable rejections:

1. REMIND YOURSELF THAT YOU HAVE NOTHING TO LOSE

To aid in overcoming the fear of rejection, Jack Canfield, author of *The Success Principles*, says to remind yourself that you have nothing to lose. For instance, let's say you decided to apply to Harvard and got rejected. You weren't in Harvard before you applied, and you aren't in Harvard after you applied. Your life didn't get worse; it stayed the same. You haven't actually lost anything (except a nominal application fee). You have spent your whole life not going to Harvard, so you know exactly how to handle that.

2. SEPARATE YOURSELF EMOTIONALLY FROM YOUR INVESTING

If you don't emotionally divorce yourself from the offers

you make as an investor, it is much easier to let critical words get you down. Just keep in mind that this is simply the offer that makes financial sense to you. It is not part of you; it's just your numbers. Viewing the situation this way makes it so you aren't emotionally attached to your offer.

3. JUST SAY "NEXT!"

Jack Canfield wrote the following in *The Success Principles*:

> Get used to the idea there is going to be a lot of rejection along the way to the gold ring. The secret to success is not to give up. When someone says no, you say, "Next!" Keep on asking. When Colonel Harlan Sanders left home with his pressure cooker and his special recipe for cooking southern fried chicken, he received over 300 rejections before he found someone to believe in his dream. Because he was rejected over 300 times, there are now over 11,000 KFC restaurants in eighty countries around the world.[4]

When your offer is rejected, rather than fuming about it, the best question to ask is, "What seller should we try next?"

4. IT'S A NUMBERS GAME

When it comes right down to it, getting an offer accepted is a crapshoot. You must find a seller who is willing to sell for

---

4   Jack Canfield, *The Success Principles* (New York: Harper Collins, 2006): 148.

significantly less than market value. Most of them simply won't want to do that. Often it just takes repeated offers to many sellers to get someone to say yes. It can really be a numbers game.

5. THE MOST SUCCESSFUL INVESTORS GET REJECTED THE MOST OFTEN

Sometimes there exists a false notion that those who have a lot going on are extremely gifted negotiators. In most cases, this is completely wrong; the most successful investors are the ones who are submitting tons of offers. They are getting rejected more frequently as well. Rejection is quite common, even for the most successful real estate investors.

This principle applies in the writing field as well. Below is a list of some well-known books and how many times the authors were each rejected before finally being published:[5]

Jonathan Livingston Seagull by Richard Bach: 140 rejections

Gone with the Wind by Margaret Mitchell: 38 rejections

Carrie by Stephen King: 30 rejections

Watership Down by Richard Adams: 26 rejections

---

5   Stephen Fraser, "Jilted Authors Put Rejection Letters behind Them—by Printing Them on Toilet Paper," *Cision*, September 27, 2005, https://www.prweb.com/releases/2005/09/prweb290039.htm.

Harry Potter by JK Rowling: 12 rejections (Rowling is vague on the number of rejections she got, saying, "I'm not sure if it was a dozen, but it was plenty.")

English novelist John Creasey received 763 rejection letters before publishing 564 books. You get the picture. These authors are now famous because they pushed through the rejection and kept trying. For instance, Stephen King got discouraged while writing *Carrie* and threw out his first few pages. His wife rescued the pages from the trash, wiped off the cigarette ashes, and urged him to stick with it.[6] So much of success is being persistent.

6. VIEW REJECTION AS PRICELESS FEEDBACK

A seller's feedback is an invaluable resource that has helped me to drastically improve my game as a negotiator. Jack Canfield recommends viewing "negative feedback as information about 'improvement opportunities'"[7] and suggests there are three ways of responding to feedback that doesn't work. These are caving in and quitting, getting mad at the source of the feedback, or ignoring the feedback. These ineffective strategies for dealing with negative feedback may help you feel better for the moment. But none of them will help you in the long term. Remember, you have an

6   Stephen King, "Stephen King: How I Wrote *Carrie*," *Guardian*, April 4, 2014, http://www.theguardian.com/books/2014/apr/04/stephen-king-how-i-wrote-carrie-horror.

7   Canfield, *The Success Principles*, 153.

invaluable learning resource at your fingertips every time you get rejected.

KEY TAKEAWAYS

How you handle rejection is a key indicator for how successful you will be in real estate, for several reasons. If you fear failure, you will be less inclined to talk to sellers and less likely to make offers. A fear of failure may also prevent you from following up and reconnecting with a seller who previously rejected you but who is now ready to sell.

To overcome your fear and deal with rejection, remind yourself you are no worse off for trying. Emotionally separate yourself from your work and think "Next!" when you get rejected, and realize it's just a numbers game. Keep in mind that the most successful investors actually get rejected the most, and you can become a better negotiator every time you fail. Nobody likes rejection, but the true test of a great investor is not whether they are rejected or even how often rejection comes. The true test of success is what they do in reaction to rejection.

While rejection and failure are part of the process, my goal is to set you up for success as much as possible. In the next chapter, I will take you through some of the most common pitfalls, so you can avoid mistakes you don't need to make.

TAKE ACTION EXERCISE: DEALING WITH REJECTION

(Download a printable version at www.lambertbonus.com.)

1. Write about one or two things you found most helpful in this chapter that you want to apply to your career.

2. Based on what you have read in this chapter, what are the areas in which fear of rejection is limiting you the most?

3. What can you do to minimize the harmful effects of rejection in your life?

4. Rejection can actually be beneficial if you handle it the right way. Write about ways you have benefited from a past rejection.

CHAPTER 21

PITFALLS OF THE NEW REAL ESTATE INVESTOR

I never want to paint the picture that real estate is all rainbows and butterflies. No, you've got to have some guts and stamina to problem-solve tough situations from time to time.

I do a lot of *Subject To* and seller-financing deals, and they've made me a good amount of money. Something that almost never happens is the bank calling the note due, but that's exactly what happened on one of my properties. To make matters worse, I had already sold the property on seller financing to someone else. What a pickle!

First, I tried to put the original seller back on the title, but he had already incurred several judgments that would have attached to the property. A no go.

Next, I checked to see if the couple I sold the property to would sell or refinance it. This would pay both the bank and me off. They wanted a $30,000 discount to do that for me. A no go.

Finally, I took a good look at my credit, which had been in the toilet for the past three years because I maxed out 0 percent interest credit cards. However, I'd joined a business-credit-building program and paid off a few hundred thousand in credit card debt. My score had barely recovered to the point that I could refinance the property in my name.

The good news is that when I closed on the refinance, I was able to:

1. Pull out every cent of my equity from the property— right around $60,000, which I could then use to buy more properties!
2. Maintain a monthly cash flow of a few hundred a month, which is an infinite return, since I don't have a penny in the deal anymore.
3. Get another needed mortgage on my credit, which boosts my future business-credit opportunities.

In the end, this challenge was resolved through persistent solution-seeking. Everything turned out better than I could have hoped for!

The moral of this story is that if you get stuck in a bad situation, keep pushing forward until you find a solution. While you can often work your way out of a challenge, if you want to maximize your success in this industry, it's best to avoid getting into bad situations in the first place. I've already covered some of the most common pitfalls in previous chapters, like prioritizing getting out of debt (chapter 2), doing too much yourself and not delegating (chapter 4), using only your own money (chapter 7), and giving up too quickly when rejected (chapter 20). In this current chapter, I'll describe some of the other common pitfalls new investors fall into and the mindsets you need to avoid them.

FAILURE TO ANALYZE AND INCORPORATE ALL COSTS

New investors don't know what they don't know, and this includes all the costs of doing a deal. For example, I can't tell you how many of my elite investor team members have brought me something they thought was a deal. Here's a common scenario: it was listed for $30,000 below market value, so they thought it was a deal. If my elite investor team member bought such a deal, they would find out the rehab cost alone was $30,000, the selling costs were

$12,000, and the money costs were $14,000. So, instead of making a profit, they'd be losing $26,000 if everything went perfectly.

Solution. Adopt a mindset that you don't know what you don't know. It's always better to overestimate costs and leave wiggle room in your profit. A great rule of thumb to quickly analyze what you can offer is the formula ARV (after repair value) times 0.75 minus repair costs. This formula takes into account making a 10 percent profit and your selling and money costs. You're going to want to carefully get all costs included eventually, but this will give you a rough estimate.

FAILURE TO DO DUE DILIGENCE

New investors often buy on emotion. Many times, they don't realize all the things to look out for and to avoid when doing due diligence. Some of the items they might find will really turn a decent deal into a total lemon.

Solution. The mindset you need is that due diligence isn't a good idea; it's a *requirement*, and it should be left to the professionals. The most important due diligence is the title work. If you bought a property, planning to make $30,000, and then you found out there was a $70,000 tax lien on the property, suddenly you're in a world of hurt. Get the title work done. Methamphetamines at a property is another really important part of due diligence, and it can cost quite a bit to clean up. Foundation problems can be devastating, as are mold, asbestos, roof issues, sewer issues, and the list goes on.

Don't try to become a pro at identifying all the potential red flags. Rather, it's best to always hire a professional inspector to do what they specialize in. If you have the property under contract, it is definitely worth paying for a report. Not only could you avoid serious issues, but you can use it as leverage with the seller to lower the price even further (as discussed in chapter 13).

FAILURE TO GET TRAINING

A lot of investors are do-it-yourselfers who want to save every penny they can. They may have spent over $100,000 on a college education, but they're unwilling to invest even a fraction of that to educate themselves in real estate. I'm not sure why some people look at becoming a real estate investor as something that doesn't need formal training. It isn't any different than other professions. It requires an education. I've heard it said many times: "I'd rather put money down for my first property than pay for education." Unfortunately, you usually have to pay for an education one way or another—either through formal training programs or through the school of hard knocks. The school of hard knocks is a pretty rough teacher, and it may prevent you from continuing on to your second deal. I want people to build true wealth, not to get a property or two, and that takes education.

Solution. Get out of the "get rich quick" mindset and adopt a long-term wealth mindset. To reach your financial freedom goals, you will need to invest in yourself. Search for a training program that contains all three elements of optimizing success, as detailed in chapter 1: education, mentorship, and community. Each plays a crucial role in your development and growth. Note that online instructional videos are no substitute for education, as they don't provide all the details you need. Make sure you find an educational program that provides both a depth and a breadth of explanation. Since you're building wealth, you ideally need not just classes about real estate, but also knowledge on areas of finance that intersect with real estate. Subjects could include taxes, credit, business credit, home equity credit lines, and becoming your own bank.

FAILURE TO COLLABORATE

Some new investors get into a scarcity mindset. They want to keep every penny of profit for themselves, and they shoot themselves in the foot. My dad always told me 50 percent of something is *far* better than 100 percent of nothing, which is what these investors often get. You can get so many more deals going if you synergize and team up with other people.

Of the six main parts of a deal as described in chapter 9, you only need to get two or three of them down to add a great deal of value in a partnership.

Henry Ford revolutionized America with his assembly line idea. He showed that rather than knowing how to assemble an entire car, each worker could specialize and gain expertise in one skill. By collaborating, these workers were able to build a Model T every twenty-four seconds. The quality was far better, too, since each person got really good at their specialty. Again, collaborating and masterminding with other investors will be crucial for your success. You will need to delegate if you want true time freedom.

Solution. Don't hesitate to collaborate with other real estate professionals. Avoid falling into a scarcity mindset where you'll feel like you are competing against other investors for a limited number of deals. This makes you want to try to keep quiet on information about the property rather than seeking feedback and help from other investors. By doing this, you may be missing key information that would help you avoid a deal you really shouldn't be doing. There are enough deals and profits to go around, so you don't need to keep every penny of profit for yourself. What you really need is an experienced partner to guide you through the transaction, and that's what you gain when you collaborate or split deals. Adopt an abundance mindset!

KEY TAKEAWAYS

There are many potential pitfalls new investors fall into, but if you can learn how to accurately analyze all the costs of a deal, do first-rate due diligence, acquire quality training, and collaborate, you'll be well on your way to absolutely crushing it! The key to avoiding these pitfalls is often to simply change your mindset.

To take things one step further, in the next chapter, I'll detail what it takes to have the mindset of a millionaire investor!

TAKE ACTION EXERCISE: COMMON PITFALLS

(Download a printable version at www.lambertbonus.com.)

1. Write about one or two things you found most helpful in this chapter that you want to apply to your career.

2. What pitfall do you think you might be most susceptible to?

3. What are some steps you can take to avoid this pitfall?

4. How would you rate yourself on a scale from one (scarcity mindset) to ten (complete abundance mindset)? What will you do to gain a more abundant mindset?

CHAPTER 22

THE MINDSET OF A MILLIONAIRE INVESTOR

Edmund decided to create a vision board. He thought about what he really wanted to accomplish in real estate and in life. He selected photos that illustrated his dreams. He was shocked at how suddenly he was accomplishing so much of what he put on his vision board. He bought four rentals, he flipped five houses, and he started going on amazing trips with his family.

The only thing that had changed was his mindset. By placing his compelling vision of the future at the forefront of his mind, he was making it happen. Remember, becoming very clear on what you want in your life is the *first* step to making it all happen.

I believe that a winning mindset accounts for 80 percent of one's success in life. You'll need to cultivate this daily to succeed in real estate investing. The goal of this chapter is to help you internalize the core aspects of a millionaire mindset that will lead you to achieve more than you thought possible in real estate.

INVEST IN YOURSELF

I've now made well over one hundred property investments. Many have brought me astronomical rates of return in a short period of time. I've put money in mutual funds, bonds, life insurance, retirement accounts, and so on. Want to know what has been my best investment of all? The time and money I have invested in myself.

I mentioned this briefly in the prior chapter, but it's so important, it's worth bringing up again. You absolutely must invest in yourself. The books I've read and the workshops I've attended have helped cleanse my mind of self-doubt and limiting beliefs. They have taught me how to dream big. I've taken training courses on sales and communication, classes on financial literacy, parenting workshops, fitness coaching, and so on, and they were all worth every penny! When I want to improve or develop a skill for my life or business, I find a person who is much better than I am, and I pay them to mentor and teach me everything they can on the topic.

As we grow and develop, we can add more value to others, and when we give value to others, we get rewarded with more money to invest even more in ourselves. It's an upward spiral. Most importantly, the better you become, the more human beings you can influence for good, making a true difference in the world. I believe nothing makes God happier than to watch all of us grow, progress, and help each other in this journey of life.

PERSISTENCE

One time, I was trying to help someone avoid foreclosure and buy their house before it was auctioned off. I was told it was too late to stop the auction, but I just kept trying. I got my title company to stay late on Friday and even come in on Saturday to get the property signed for. On Monday, I had several bankers and lawyers tell me the $10,000 I sent them came too late. They had already sold the house to someone else at the auction. But I just kept trying. I kept calling bank employees and lawyers and emailed them all my wire transfer documents as evidence I'd sent the money *before* the auction started.

Then, the unexpected happened. They actually undid the sale and gave my partner and me the house! Months passed, and it seemed like we were never going to get the seller out of the property. He was unfortunately suffering from some mental health issues that disabled him from leaving in an appropriate manner. I just kept trying, and we finally got him out, with the help of an eviction court win and three constables who escorted him out. After rehabbing the house, we put it on the market. Nobody made an offer for three straight months, but we just kept trying.

Finally, we got five offers in a single day! I felt lots of excitement and relief when my partner and I signed and split a $100,000-plus profit! This deal took a lot of determination and willpower. We had to keep trying, even when our prospects for success looked bleak. If you can stick to it and keep trying, you can reap great rewards in whatever your endeavor!

Persistence is perhaps the most important mindset to cultivate as a real estate investor. You just have to keep pushing forward and tenaciously go after your goals until you reach them. I now have helped hundreds of people in their real estate journey. The ones who have been far and away the most successful are the ones who have consistently shown up to learn and take action. I know you can too!

MIRACLE MORNING

Tony Robbins suggests 80 percent of the success you will have in this life lies in your mind. We must condition ourselves daily for the success we desire through beginning each day in a peak state or a state of optimal productivity.

I've found the best way for me to achieve a peak state is through a miracle morning. I'd strongly recommend the book *Miracle Morning* by Hal Elrod. Here's a summary of the core parts of the miracle morning he describes with the acronym SAVERS:

Silence. Starting out with silence is powerful. Focus on the breath through meditation. This can get you started with powerful focus and concentration. I recommend the online app Headspace for guided meditation that will walk you through every step.

Affirmations. Create a list of statements written in the present tense that reflect your goals and desires. Include what you're trying to achieve, not just in finances but in the rest of your life as well. "I am a decamillionaire," "I have $500,000 in reserves," "I am a loving parent," "I spend quality time with my kids each day," are examples of some of my affirmations. Repeat these affirmations aloud to yourself every day and you will program your mind for success.

Visualization. "A picture is worth a thousand words" is a true statement because our mind works visually. Create a vision board. In the first chapter's Take Action Exercise, you described all the things you wanted to be, have, and experience as you reach for financial independence. Go to your search engine and do some image searches on the things you listed. Print them out on a color printer, perhaps with some words describing what the picture represents. Make a collage and put it in front of where you spend a lot of time, so you see it frequently.

Exercise. Your body desperately needs the enhanced oxygen from cardiovascular workouts. Your heart, mind, and soul need it too. The endorphins released as you exercise will help put you into a peak state. For the sake of limited time, I exercise while meditating, shouting out my affirmations and looking at my vision board. I pair it all together.

Reading. Another key part of mindset is the inspirational books you consume. To be a successful real estate investor, you will need to read dozens of books about sales, business, mindset, strategy, and so much more. These great books can put you in a peak state and get you mentally ready for the day as well. Don't feel like you need to read for long amounts of time. I use a listening app and actually listen to books while I'm exercising and preparing for the day.

Scribe. The final step in the SAVERS formula is scribe, writing out your thoughts and, ideally, your gratitudes. Gratitude is one of the most powerful emotions possible and can put you into a state of abundance. Writing out three things you are grateful for can set a powerful tone for your entire day.

You can do all six of these steps in thirty minutes or less. Or perhaps you don't end up doing every step of the SAVERS formula. You can make it your own.

KEY TAKEAWAYS

To build the mindset of a millionaire investor, invest in yourself, be persistent, and create a "miracle morning" routine. Even pros fall into the trap of thinking they know everything they need, but the greatest investment you can make is in yourself and your education. It's also important to not let discouragement overcome you. The greatest real estate investors are the ones who persist despite every challenge that presents itself. Finally, morning rituals and habits are crucial for your success. I can't tell you how important this is for your ultimate success as an investor. Your day is made or broken before 9:00 a.m.

CONCLUSION

I had always wanted to go to Thailand ever since I can remember, but with five children, it was going to cost a small fortune. It was a busy year for me in 2018, because that's when I really began to scale my business. When I made sufficient money, I decided to book our flights for this dream trip. I had a huge rush of adrenaline come over me when I bought those tickets. Planning the trip was so much more meaningful than ever before, as I could finally afford to stay in the beautiful beachside homes I'd always dreamed of.

I had told my oldest brother, when I began my real estate journey six years earlier, that I wanted to become a millionaire by the age of forty. A week before leaving on our trip, I was able to buy a few more properties. When I added up the value of all my assets minus my liabilities, I realized I had arrived. I had become a millionaire and was two years ahead of schedule! That was such an amazing feeling, it's difficult to describe.

I wrote an email to the department chair who had attempted to sabotage my career as a professor. I told him I forgave him for the pain he had caused me and thanked him for pushing me out of my comfort zone. He played an important role in getting me to where I am today. If it hadn't been for him, it's possible I never would have had the courage to make such a bold change. I'm so grateful my path took this new direction. Forgiveness is always the right answer.

Thailand was everything I had hoped for and more! We got to ride elephants, play with tigers, explore ancient ruins and Buddhist temples, fly to remote islands, and play on white-sand beaches. Our accommodations were unique and every bit as wonderful as they seemed online. We made memories there that will last a lifetime.

However, as fantastic as that was, it's hard to beat what came next—a trip to Cambodia. I became part of an organization that builds wells to provide a clean water source to poverty-stricken villagers. Before we'd left on our trip, as a family we had coordinated a clothing drive, both in my faith community and in my real estate investing community. It was so powerful to watch my children passing out bread and clothing to the children in these villages. We watched the construction crews as they dug the wells. I walked around the village with one of the chiefs, and he showed me the spot where he wanted to build a school one day. He knew learning English would give the children in his village a chance for a better life. It was so powerful to tell this chief his "one day" would be in the next few months as I wrote out a check to build a school for his village.

It's hard to describe the feeling that came over me when the well was completed and we gathered with the villagers to commemorate the moment. One of the mothers approached me and gave me a huge hug. She said, "I can't thank you enough for providing clothes, food, a source of clean drinking water for my family, and an education for my children. We will never forget you!"

It's an amazing feeling to become a millionaire, to move into a nine-thousand-square-foot mansion, and to have the time and money freedom to travel three months of the year with my family. Yet it will be hard to top the outpouring of love I felt in that remote village in Cambodia. I knew all my work flipping and renting houses allowed me to make a true, long-lasting impact on these people. It's all about paying it forward!

One of my core goals in writing this book is to create a community of thousands of successful, philanthropic real estate millionaires who attain the financial independence they seek for their family. Then we can all pay it forward to bless many people throughout the world.

As I conclude this book, I sincerely hope you have received incredible value. I encourage you to regularly reflect on your financial independence goals and to think about what your financial independence would mean not just for you and your family, but for the world. If you are in a situation like I was in which you are struggling with no money, no fun, no freedom, or no impact, it's time to take action. Instead of living a passive life on active income, flip the script. With real estate investing, you can build passive income, achieve financial independence, and begin living the active life you've always wanted.

ABOUT THE AUTHOR

NATE LAMBERT is a real estate investor, a world traveler of forty-five countries and counting, a psychology PhD, the father of five boys, a philanthropist, and an international speaker.

He flips roughly twenty houses annually and has owned over fifty rental properties—numbers that continue to grow every year. He has helped thousands of people in forty-seven states find profitable real estate deals. His goal is to achieve over $100,000 per month in passive income and to help tens of thousands of people become real estate millionaires—including you.